To. Professor Charles S. Braden
with very good and sincere
wishes from the author

Gerald B Bryan

September 13, 1944

PSYCHIC DICTATORSHIP IN AMERICA

PSYCHIC

DICTATORSHIP

IN

AMERICA

by GERALD B. BRYAN

TRUTH RESEARCH PUBLICATIONS
456 So. Western Ave., Los Angeles, California

PUBLISHER'S NOTE

Just before this book came off the press the amazing cult which it exposes was indicted by the Federal Grand Jury at Los Angeles on charges of fraudulent use of the mails. We quote below excerpts from *Associated Press Dispatch* of July 24, 1940:

"A federal grand jury today indicted 24 leaders of the "I AM" Foundation, a nationwide movement reported to have attracted a million converts, on charges of fraudulent use of the mails.

"Testimony by postal inspectors resulted in 16 counts of misuse of the mails and one count of conspiracy . . .

"Norman Neukom, assistant United States attorney who presented the case to the grand jury, said the "I AM" cultists had collected close to $3,000,000 since the movement's inception in 1930."

PSYCHIC DICTATORSHIP IN AMERICA reveals heretofore unpublished and startling facts about this subversive cult.

PREFACE

This is a history and psychological study of one of America's most astounding cults. An incredible story of the strangest dictatorship now current in our land.

It recounts how an unseen, psychic potentate dominates the minds and actions of thousands of patriotic American citizens, who, today, meet in closed, secret study-groups in most of the cities throughout the United States.

It relates how two self-styled "Accredited Messengers" of invisible "Masters" rose from obscurity to fame and fortune by bringing forth a new Messiah—allegedly an actual historical character who had considerable political influence in Europe during the middle of the 18th century.

But this book is intended to be more than just an interesting history of a curious faith, or recital of an ever-recurring Messianic complex. It is a study of strange psychological forces revealed mainly through the history of a single subversive cult, but which have their influence also on other movements operating in America today.

It shows, in these days when panaceas parade the land and people reach out for straws to save themselves, how American ideals of freedom and independence are being supplanted by a slavish dependence upon odd sorts of deliverances. And oddest perhaps of all current movements, and loaded with special brands of psychological and political dynamite, is the cult this book exposes.

Similar movements, no doubt, have occurred in the past, but none of them has shown the sheer audacity and careless dealing with the truth as the one whose incredible and fantastic history is here recorded—a recital which serves so well to typify, in some respects, the peculiar history of the time through which America today is passing.

The author hopes that its amazing story will serve to reveal subversive psychological influences which are producing widespread mental confusion in the United States, from which some form of political despotism may sprout and jeopardize constitutional principles of Freedom and Liberty upon which this nation is founded.

It is his hope, too, that such a history and study will be an example and warning should, now or at any future time, other subversive movements, using similar psychological methods of regimentating the minds of credulous people, get underway in America.

To those who after reading this book find sad disillusionment concerning a movement which so long has held their earnest and devoted allegiance, the author can only express the wish to see them happily using their aspirations and talents elsewhere in God's great kingdom. With many, no doubt, there will be felt a glad release, a sense of freedom to be cut loose from servile obedience to pretended "Masters," to be freed from the hypnotic domination of a *"Psychic Dictatorship."*

GERALD B. BRYAN

Los Angeles, California.
July, 1940.

CONTENTS

Contents—*Continued*

CHAPTER 1

AMERICA TURNS TO THE "MIGHTY I AM"

Along the boulevard the crowd gathers in front of the well-lighted building.

"This must be the place," you say to yourself, falling in line with others hurrying along the street.

A friend has been urging you to attend, and last night's radio broadcast has further intrigued your interest. So here you are.

It is early, but already nearby parking lots are filled. Nicely dressed men and women exchange greetings as they hurry to get into the meeting, but some are rather curiously attired. A woman swishes by in a long white gown which trails the ground. Another goes by in flaming violet. One in golden yellow. A wheel chair bearing a cripple is being pushed through one of the entrances.

"Registration cards at window to the right!" someone announces. Soon, with one in your hand, you edge through the crowd and are in the brilliantly lighted auditorium.

A courteous white-robed attendant greets you with a smile, presenting you with a colorful song book and a little envelope marked "I Am Love Gift."

"God bless you," she says.

Taken a bit by surprise, you return the greeting. A male usher, dressed nattily in a white suit, conducts you officiously down the aisle.

Ensconced in a comfortable seat and still holding on to the little love gift envelope and the peach-colored song book, you look around.

The auditorium already is well filled and presents a colorful effect with its gathering of the faithful in their habiliments of pinks and purples and yellows and other shades and hues of color. The women are in predominance, but the men, mostly dressed in white, are far from being inconspicuous. Good-looking male ushers, all in dressy white, stand at attention at certain points in the aisles, or politely conduct the incoming streams of people to their seats.

You hear music and sit back relaxed, waiting for the lecture to begin. But there seems to be no hurry about it. Like a gala event, the crowds have assembled long before the scheduled appearance of the speakers.

A peace settles over you, but not the sleepy kind. The atmosphere around you is vibrant with expectancy.

The stage is banked with gorgeous flowers. You can almost imagine the smell of their fragrance. Makes you think of the last wedding or funeral you attended. Yet the scene before you is different from either.

A forest of pine trees at the extreme ends of the stage lures you into dreamy recollections. Colored lights play between the trees. Reminds you of Christmas.

In the center of the stage is a large colorful chart of two human figures, one placed above the other. The upper figure, resplendent in its glory of many colors, has radiating streamers like a miniature borealis. The lower one is less spectacular perhaps, and is bathed in a constant flow of radiations which stream up from the feet. This you later learn is the *"Violet Consuming Flame,"* a purifying and destroying element. Oddly enough, this human figure and its restless cloud of violet are enclosed in a white outline resembling a milk bottle.

The complete ensemble—the heavenly figure above and the more human one below—you later learn is the *"Chart of the Presence."* An absolute essential in this cult's system of salvation.

Shrouded in a bower of flowers to your left, by the side of the central chart, is an easel and picture. This you make out is the portrait of Jesus. A mild-visaged creation, with marcel-waved hair and beard.

To your right on the other side of the chart is a companion picture, also in its bower of flowers. A golden bearded and mustached gentleman with piercing eyes. This you soon learn is the "exact likeness" of the great *"Ascended Master Saint Germain."*

This bearded master with peculiar eyes seems to exert a strange fascination. You turn to the mild Jesus on your left. And now your gaze shifts to and fro like a pendulum between the two portraits. A queer feeling settles over you.

To break it, you look at the central chart with its two human figures and radiating streamers. Your eyes now travel perpendicularly up from the lower figure to the upper one, and back again. Again that peculiar feeling. You wonder about it.

The sudden appearance of someone on the stage interrupts your contemplations.

It is a man dressed in dazzling white. Advancing toward the footlights, he holds up his hands in greeting. He is now at the microphone radiating his love and blessings. You settle back in your seat again, for he is but an announcer, not the prime mover of the show.

It is a first night, and there is much exchange of greetings. He holds up telegrams from other cities in the United States. There are greetings from Canada, and even a cablegram. He reads some of them. They all send love and blessings to the new class which has just started. The announcer goes on to say that marvelous happenings took place at the class just closed in the last city visited. But this one, he says, is simply to be *"Transcendent!"*

"Blessed Saint Germain has promised it," he adds, lifting his eyes heavenward with awe and reverence. And a hush settles over the audience.

Not knowing just where to look for Saint Germain's apparition, your eyes travel to his bearded and mustached portrait on the stage to your right. His eyes hold your attention. With an effort you switch to the portrait of Jesus, and you realize with a start that so far everything has centered around the *"Mighty Master Saint Germain."* You cannot help but wonder at it.

Specific references are now being made to the "I Am Love Gift Boxes" located at the rear of the auditorium. You find later that they are very conveniently and advantageously placed for the reception of the little "Love Gift" envelope you hold in your hand.

"Dear ones!" says the announcer earnestly. *"Blessed Mr. and Mrs. Ballard* do not need these offerings; they are merely for you beloved students to 'open up channels' for blessings from the great Ascended Masters."

The eyes of the announcer again look heavenward as though showers of blessings had already accompanied this reference to the unseen "Masters."

"Unless you give freely,' he adds, still very earnestly, "you cannot receive." Then very emphatically, "That is the Ascended Master's law of life!"

The smooth-voiced announcer still runs on in his talk as though playing for time. You wonder when the scheduled lecturers will appear on the stage. There seems to be no hurry about it so far as the announcer is concerned. But you now want ever so much to see and hear the *"Accredited Messengers of the Great Ascended Master Saint Germain"*—which you remember was the way the lecturers were referred to over the radio.

References are now being made to the need of working and "decreeing" for the United States of America and the Constitution.

"We must save America!" says the announcer. You learn there are "vicious forces" within her borders and without. These are all to be destroyed! They are to be

"blasted" from the face of the earth by the "decrees" of the students. Saint Germain, the mighty "Cosmic Master," has commanded it!

Like other movements which have as their credo the "saving of America," the flag of the American republic is displayed prominently on the stage. But you notice there are *two* large flags on the stage instead of the customary one. You think Saint Germain's Americanism leans a little backward here. Also, little American flags are displayed prominently on the lapels and white dresses of men and women in the audience. The man on the stage has his little flag too. Everywhere there seem to be flags—little stripes of red and white and rectangles of blue—adding more color and sentiment to a gala event.

But you soon learn to your surprise that the color red is simply intolerable to Saint Germain and his "Accredited Messengers." It is the color of the communists and all that is vicious, says the announcer. "You students should not wear it. . . . No Ascended Master ever uses it." The only exception seems to be the flag of our country.

"Some day, however," the announcer quotes Saint Germain as saying, "when the Ascended Masters take charge of the affairs of this country, there will be *gold stripes* instead of red ones in the flag of the new American republic!"

"This is not a religion," the announcer adds, "but a patriotic movement."

He goes on to extol the "marvelous" patriotic work of the *"Minute Men of Saint Germain."* This you learn is a men's patriotic organization within the parent body which has dedicated itself to fly to the rescue of America, as did the minute men of 1776.

You learn also of the activities of the *"Daughters of Light,"* a sort of ladies auxiliary, with similar patriotic aims and purposes.

The audience you observe is accepting all this in perfect peace and contentment. They evidently have heard it many times before, and it is easy for them and the announcer to go through it again. Tolerant of the easy and lulling voice of the announcer, they nevertheless appear to be expectantly waiting, waiting for something to happen.

You, too, sit back complacently; but you do wonder about such things as the gold stripes in the new American flag—and just when it will be that the "Ascended Masters" will take over the affairs of the country.

In the midst of thinking about all of this, suddenly there is a resounding note on the pipe organ and a trumpet sounds from back stage. The audience is rising to its feet almost in a body. Rather uncertain what to do, you rise also. There seems to be nothing else to do. You don't want to be stared at.

Sweeping forward on the stage come the three individuals responsible for all this fanfare. The great moment is here!

A woman, blond, radiant, and sparkling with jewels, dressed as for the opera, takes the center of the stage and showers the audience with her love.

A gray-haired man of about sixty attired in a white tuxedo, smiles beatifically at the audience and bows with her. Diamonds flash from his hands and other parts of his person.

A youth, dressed also in white, the son of this startling couple, stands at a sort of diffident attention on the stage while all this is going on. He seems for the moment not to be a part of the performance.

With the electric appearance of Saint Germain's "Accredited Messengers" on the stage all is changed. The audience comes to life. It is galvanized into action. Soon, led by this gorgeously-gowned, throaty-voiced blond woman, who has taken the center of the stage, *"decrees"* are being shouted in unison throughout the crowded auditorium.

Staccato-like sentences are hurled into the atmosphere. . . . Hands are raised. . . . Thoughts are sent sizzling through the auditorium. One can imagine them going like projectiles to their destination.

There is perfect timing and rhythm in the *"hurling forth"* of these decrees. Certain it is that these people are in deadly earnest. The spirit of the mob prevails, orderly, but easily recognized for what it is—*mass hypnosis*—concentrated and directed by one mind, one power, one overweening personality, psychic and unreasoning in its effect.

And so amidst applause, blessings, and "decrees," another *"Mighty I AM"* class is now well under way. It will run for ten full days, or perhaps seventeen, both afternoon and evening, and part of it will be broadcast to listening thousands beyond the big city.

The author leaves the reader with this picture, and will pass on to the moving series of events that led up to such an assemblage, which will explain, he hopes, the idolatrous devotion of the large and applauding audience for these people, and why so many patriotic Americans have embraced so earnestly and so vociferously the strange cult of the "Mighty I AM."*

---

*The author hopes that the reader will bear in mind that any criticism of the so-called "Mighty I AM" instruction of Guy and Edna Ballard is directed at this cult's false conception and misuse of the "I AM" philosophy and **not** at the "I AM" itself, which, to many, is a symbol of the "Higher Self," the **God Within.** It is regretable that so often a legitimate philosophy is made to bear the burden of illegitimate use.

CHAPTER 2

STREAMLINE BEGINNINGS

At a modest brick bungalow, 1620 East 84th Place, Chicago, there occurred during the fall of 1932 a series of assertedly miraculous happenings, out of which has arisen the most fantastic and extravagant spiritualistic movement in American history.

Some form of spiritualistic communication has always been the belief and hope of the human race. Sometimes such a belief has been tempered with reason and common sense. All too often, however, it has been made to flare into something analogous to a raging forest fire, periodically sweeping certain sections of the country, preying upon credulous minds, and laying waste a lot of mental timber of promise.

Such has been the result of the spiritualistic phenomena which assertedly took place in the red brick bungalow on 84th Place in old Chicago, and which during the last few years has flared into a psychic conflagration so widespread and intense that it should be of considerable interest to psychologists and psychiatrists who deal in strange behaviorisms of the human mind, as well as to politicians who astutely watch the current of human emotion, that they may the better obtain power and authority in the land.

In the history of the American colonies, and even in more recent times, there are other instances of such psychic movements, but never, however, on such a flamboyant and extravagant a scale as this present-day cult.

Nearly a hundred years ago, at another little house,

now historically famous as the "*Fox Cottage at Hydes-ville, New York,*" there similarly occurred certain psychic phenomena credited with having given birth to spiritualism in America.

This humble house, occupied by honest John Fox, his wife, and their two little children, became what was popularly known in that day as "haunted." Here there began a remarkable series of psychic "rappings" and "knockings" which were destined to be heard throughout the United States of that day, and are still being heard in thousands of seances throughout the country.

But in this latter-day happening which assertedly occurred in an equally unpretentious house, although not considered "haunted," this ancient and primitive belief in the supernormal has taken wings on a flight of fancy far beyond that of the humble happenings at the cottage home of the little Fox sisters. For this later happening deals not with spirit "raps" and "knocks," but with distinctly more modern and streamlined methods of communicating with the other side of life.

In short, instead of having ordinary "spirit guides" and commonplace "ghosts" of departed relatives giving the usual type of spirit messages, we now have, reportedly, great and mighty "*Ascended Masters*" speaking audibly over a dazzling "LIGHT AND SOUND RAY!"

Foremost among the "Masters" who speak audibly over this streamlined "Light and Sound Ray" is the great "*Ascended Master Saint Germain,*" who is alleged to have been the same mysterious personage whom history records as the *Comte de St. Germain*—a man who in the 18th century had wide political influence, and was adviser to Louis XV of France and some other potentates of that day.

Thus the world moves on; and today the disciples of the new cult can sit comfortably at home by their own radios listening to inspired fireside chats from this 18th-century Count, telling about the state of the nation and the world, or they may read his "Light and Sound Ray" *discourses,* all printed and duly copyrighted in seven large green-colored books!

The first of these books has the alluring title: *"Unveiled Mysteries,"* wherein is described how the hero, a *Mr. Godfre Ray King,* meets in the fall of 1930 the Comte de St. Germain *in person* on the side of a California mountain.

Godfre Ray King, we later learn is none other than *Guy W. Ballard,* co-originator of the Mighty I AM cult; and, according to this book, he *"had been sent on government business to a little town situated at the foot of the mountain."* (p. 1, "Unveiled Mysteries.") *

While there, according to his account, he occupied his leisure time trying to unravel a strange rumor concerning an alleged Occult Brotherhood said to be domiciled in the mountain fastnesses of *Mt. Shasta*—California's own "Mystic Mountain."

One day on one of his alleged rambles around Mt. Shasta, he stopped at a mountain spring for a drink. Cup in hand, he knelt down to fill it when something like an "electric current" passed through his body from head to foot.

Looking up, he saw "no ordinary person."

"Drink this," said the mysterious stranger, handing him a cup filled with a rich, creamy liquid. Very trustfully, Ballard did so—and he was never quite the same afterwards.

A few moments later the stranger was demonstrating his gold-making abilities to Ballard.

"See!" said the mysterious one, "I have but to hold out

---

*Please note the following abbreviations used in this book:

Unveiled Mysteries	.........U.M.	Ascended Master Discourses	..A.M.D.
The Magic Presence	.........M.P.	Ascended Master Light	.........A.M.L.
The "I AM" Discourses	........D.	Voice of the I AM	..............V.
	Group Letter	................G.L.	

my hand and if I wish to use gold—gold is here."

Instantly, Ballard said, *"there lay in his palm a disc about the size of a ten dollar gold piece!"* (p.4, U.M.)

From that time on, this mysterious mountain visitor —who turns out to be none other than the great "Ascended Master Saint Germain"—reveals to his wonder-eyed disciple *more mysteries in heaven and earth* than ever dreamed of in any Shakespearean philosophy. The great "Master" takes time out from more cosmic labors to personally escort his disciple to secret retreats in America, Arabia, and India, and gets him back to his home in Chicago in time to tune in to the marvelous "Light and Sound Ray" coming through the ceiling of Ballard's modest 84th Place bungalow.

In this streamlined spiritualistic movement there are many additional marvels, of which we shall duly learn. But just now let us introduce the couple who are the self-styled "Accredited Messengers" of this Ascended Master Saint Germain, and who are responsible for a movement which is today controlling the thought, dictating the action, and winning the financial support of tens of thousands of people in the major cities throughout the United States, a movement which actually claims *"over a million earnest and devoted students."*

Inasmuch as he *claims* to have been the originator of the movement, let us present Guy W. Ballard first. However, his good wife, Edna Wheeler Ballard, is far from being backward in her claims and activities, and one can easily gather the impression from the way the show is handled that the set-up is more of a matriarchy than a patriarchy.

GUY GEORGE WASHINGTON GODFRE RAY KING BALLARD is a tall, meticulously dressed man of some sixty years of age, usually attired in an immaculate white suit, over which, for variety, he sometimes very effectively drapes a long indigo-blue cape with shiny white satin lining, or sometimes a full-length all-white one.*

In the glare of the footlights there is much sparkle of jewels from rings and tie pin as he bows and gesticulates before his audiences.

Pale, deep-set blue eyes look out below a slanting forehead topped by grey hair, well-groomed and combed straight back as if flattened out by the wind, giving the impression of a bird in flight. A well-formed eagle-like nose and thin underjaw adds to this impression of flight into the empyrean.

In short, Guy Ballard gives the impression of being one of those individuals who can easily live in a world of their own, peopled by creatures and glories of their own imaginative making, but, albeit, in his case, a world sufficiently material to include and satisfy a life-long craving for corporeal comforts as well as for heavenly splendors.

Emotionally, this man of fantastic tales ranges from mannerisms of deepest humility to a crescendo of high and mighty utterances designed to show his self-claimed Messianic destiny as "Savior of America."

From an over-display of humility attitudes, garnished with such endearing expressions as "Dear Hearts" and "Beloved Ones," he will suddenly sweep into dynamic denunciations against "vicious individuals," spies, and black magicians, within and without our borders, and call on "Mighty Ascended Masters" to smite these individuals and all their works.

After such an exhibition of emotional pyrotechnics, the audience is either hypnotically leaning forward in their respective seats with delicious chills running up and down their individual spines, or else a few will register disgust at such mass-stirring heroics by getting up and leaving the auditorium.

---

*The first and second chapters in this book, as well as some of the others, were written BEFORE the so-called "Ascension" of Guy Ballard. However, we publish the material as written, and have retained the PRESENT tense, even though later history may now place some of the events in the past tense.

One thing is certain: This man, in his eagle-like flights of fancy and sweeping denunciations of so-called vicious individuals, has the power not only to hypnotize himself as to the truth of what he is saying, but he can, it seems, make his audience believe in the green cheese story of the moon—or its occult parallel.

The play of his emotions up and down the scale tends to keep his audiences in proper emotional trim—on their psychic toes as it were—and the recital of marvels yet to come, gold, jewels, precipitated dinners, and what not, to every devoted student through the Ballard system of salvation, makes these students all too willing to be hypnotized away from their logical faculties and follow the fanciful imaginings of the master of the show.

Let us now take a look at the feminine side of the Ballard household.

EDNA ANNA WHEELER LOTUS RAY KING BALLARD, known also as *"Little Dynamite"* to her psychic master and also as *"Chanera,"* are names which perhaps fit all the characteristics of this dynamic personality.

Years ago, before later and more euphonious names were born, she was simply Edna Wheeler Ballard, a concert harpist, a vaudeville trouper, a clerk in an occult book store, or sometimes just a housewife, varied at times by trips to the mountain tops with her gold-seeking husband and infant son, looking for the ever-eluding pot of gold (the Ballard gold mines we will learn about) at the end of the rainbow.

As simply Edna, she was like most other people struggling along through life. There was a child to raise, hospital and dental bills to pay, and the rent came around all too soon. But the restless god of ambition within her did not want it that way. It wanted power, glory, diamonds, gold, and a luxury such as attributed to fabled rulers of old. To all these besetting desires her early friends will attest.

Is it any wonder, therefore, that these ambitions should not have been outpictured some time in some tangible way? Particularly so, when it is realized that she planned, worked, and schemed for them instead of doing a lot of metaphysical wishful thinking.

A dynamic, authoritative, battling kind of person, Edna Ballard rules her "Mighty I AM" family with all the command of an Amazonian chieftain. Appropriately, therefore, may she be called *"Little Dynamite,"* the name bestowed upon her by the mighty "Ascended Master Saint Germain."

Viewed from afar, and in the soft radiance of the usual Ballard stage setting, Edna's appearance may be rather much in her favor. There is a certain grace about her figure and the rhythmic movements of her arms as she issues her decrees. Her gowns, ornate and overdone, are the envy of her women audiences and a source of wonder and admiration no doubt to some of the men. Sparkling rings and bracelets flash showers of light over her audiences. Diamond tiaras, overhanging corsages, expensive furs, gorgeous new gowns, their long trains sweeping the stage floor, all this is but an inadequate description of the complete ensemble.

And so, today, Lotus Ray King Ballard, having achieved in some degree the desires and ambitions of a frustrated Edna, has a portion of the metaphysical and phenomena-seeking world at her feet. They, too, want the things that Lotus has, and until the hypnotic spell has run its course and the thin covering of goodness and saintliness of her cult has worn down to the tinsel underneath, Lotus will hold the stage as dictator over the lives of many.

CHAPTER 3

THE "SILVER SHIRT" BACKGROUND OF BALLARDISM

Within a period of less than a decade America has seen the rise and growth of two remarkable movements which bear an odd resemblance to each other.

William Dudley Pelley's *"Silver Shirts of America,"* the first of the two movements, started originally simply as a metaphysical venture, the result of a personal psychic experience, which strangely enough, occurred while residing at a mountain cottage in California.

The Ballard *"Mighty I AM"* movement, as we have seen, started the same way, with its originator claiming his first contact with Comte de St. Germain on the side of a mountain in California.

The recent reports of the House Committee to Investigate Un-American Activities, under the chairmanship of Martin Dies of Texas, have given the Pelley Silver Shirt movement front-page headlines, revealing to the public that for years it has not been a "metaphysical" organization, as in the beginning, but is a political body which the Dies Committee believes to be un-American in that it is included in the "Nazi-Fascist groups" engaged in *"aping the methods of foreign dictators"* and attempting *"to bring about a radical change in the American form of government."* (*Associated Press Dispatch, August* 31, 1939.)

This book will reveal that the Ballard cult, too, is really a political movement and that its metaphysics, among other things, is largely engaged in an effort to bring about a weird sort of government in the United States.

The Pelley organization, as a matter of fact, supplied the *pattern* for some of the Ballard work, and evidence supporting this will soon be given. The Ballards, however, kept out of their movement the Silver Shirts' well-known hatred of the Jew, and have denounced other "enemies" instead.

There is so much similarity between the two organizations, it is well from the standpoint of psychological study and history to bring this out.

Pelley was a writer, a most clever wielder of the pen. Back in 1917 he was in the Orient on what he states to have been Christian missionary work; and after varied experiences there, he returned in 1919 to the United States to resume his writings and newspaper career. Around this time he became interested, he says, in *"Secret Service investigations,"* and claimed to have had "contacts with some of the biggest men in the Hoover administration."

Ballard in his latter years became also a writer, claims to have spent a couple of years in the Orient, and his "Secret Service connections" and his "Governmental contacts" are *most* remarkable, as we shall find.

In 1929 Pelley wrote the article which publicized his name throughout the nation. It was the story of a personal psychic experience entitled *"Seven Minutes in Eternity,"* in which he related how, while residing at a lonely bungalow in the Sierra Madre Mountains near Pasadena, California, he suddenly one night left his physical body lying on the bed and consciously soared away into that undiscovered country from whose bourn no traveler is supposed to return. But Pelley did return, and he told a graphic story of his sojourn there. Later he published messages purporting to come from "Masters," who began to direct and influence his new life work.

Similarly, Messenger Ballard, shortly after the appearance of the Pelley article, wrote up his own psychic experiences, which came to him in 1930, he said, while living at a lodge at the foot of a California mountain. He, too, left his body, and great and mighty *"Ascended"* Masters dictated marvelous discourses to him.

The *American Magazine*, which had published the Pelley story, was almost swamped, we understand, with mail in regard to it. It appears that the whole country at that time was having psychic experiences, and overnight almost Pelley had a tremendous following. All the letter-writing psychics in the land, it seems, wrote in giving their own personal experiences—and called for more from the fluent and graphic Pelley.

Obligingly, the new metaphysical leader gave his readers plenty of them, as indeed has the leader of the Mighty I AM cult which followed so soon after the start of Pelleyism.

Pelley's magazine, then named *"The New Liberator,"* was started—an artistic but rather lurid creation—and he filled it with occult articles by himself and psychic messages from great "Masters." But never were they as numerous and as notorious as the Ballard "Ascended Masters."

Gradually, Pelley's psychism took on a political coloring and flavor, and it wasn't long before he was publishing stirring ideas and plans about a *"New Government"* in America—as did Ballard shortly afterwards.

Political headquarters were established at Asheville, N. C., in 1932, and his "Foundation for Christian Economics" was started at about the time Ballard was assertedly receiving his religio-patriotic messages over the marvelous "Light and Sound Ray" at his home in Chicago.

At the beginning of 1933 Pelley started his now famous Silver Legion, and felt the egoic thrill of fascist rule over his legionnaires or *"storm troops"* organized in many parts of the country. In much the same way have the fascistic-minded leaders of the Mighty I AM cult organized their patriotic bands of *Minute Men*—the "storm troops" of the movement.

In the fall of 1936, after Pelley had recovered from certain adverse court decisions and indictments at Asheville, N. C., he organized his "Christian Party" and announced his candidacy for President of the United States *—an office to which it will be seen Ballard himself has felt himself peculiarly fitted!*

Three and a half years later, after many viscissitudes of fortune and after some months of search for him by the Dies committee, Pelley in the early part of 1940 appeared before that committee to answer certain charges allegedly to the effect that "he is a racketeer engaged in mulcting thousands of dollars annually from his fanatical and misled followers and credulous people all over the United States and Canada and certain foreign countries." *(Associated Press Dispatch*, Jan. 3, 1940.)

It is not within the scope of this book to consider whether the Dies committee was or was not justified in making the above allegations concerning Pelley. We desire merely to point out the startling parallel between these two movments and to show by actual evidence that so far as the Ballard movement is concerned the Dies committee, if it had gone into the matter, could have brought out justifiably, we believe, similar charges against Saint Germain's "Mighty I AM" movement.

We shall complete the parallel between the two movements by quoting *Associated Press Dispatch* of February 8, 1940, giving an account of Pelley's appearance before the Dies committee:

"With a trace of wistfulness, William Dudley Pelley, leader of the Silver Shirts, told the Dies committee today that if his organization had succeeded in its purposes, he 'probably' would be in charge of the government now.

"And in that case, he continued, he 'probably' would

have put into effect something resembling Adolf Hitler's policies with respect to the Jews, although he said he does not indorse Hitler's exact methods."

It is this Pelley Silver Shirt movement which Guy and Edna Ballard were particularly interested in previous to the publication of *Unveiled Mysteries*, and, as will be shown, they tried to build a foundation upon Pelley's organization in an effort to launch their own Mighty I AM movement.

In order to show this Silver Shirt background of the Ballard movement we shall now have to refer to a certain meeting which was held in the summer of 1934 at the Ballard home on 84th Place, Chicago.

To this meeting was invited the *treasurer* of the Pelley organization, some additional Pelleyites, and others interested in metaphysical and patriotic movements. It was the first regular ten-day class ever held by the Ballards, and it is important because what transpired there indicates clearly the early efforts of their invisible "Saint Germain" to lay plans for a *"New Government"* in America which was to be formed more or less along the lines previously described by Pelley in his writings.

During this ten-day class, messages from "Saint Germain" were read by Mrs. Ballard to those present, a little group of ten, who were pledged to secrecy.

One of those messages is especially significant. It is dated August 3, 1934, and we shall quote freely from it in this chapter.

In it, this so-called Saint Germain shows rather excellent understanding of human nature by the fact that he first flatters those whom he was about to use. To aid him in this, he drew on his long memory of the past, going back some seventy thousand years!

He told those flattered students of their past incarnations! He recited their marvelous achievements! They had all done great and stirring things! All of them had been associated with him before! They would even be closer to him now! They would now have a part to play in bringing the *new* civilization into America!

"These beloved students," it begins, "are all far advanced souls with whom we have been closely associated before wherein very great Light has reigned. All of this group that are here were in association in the civilization of 70,000 years ago where the Sahara Desert now is."

Saint Germain then went on in this first message to his *"Beloved Friends of Long Ago,"* to tell them about the marvelous work they did in that earlier government. He told them of their wonderful genius in the past so convincingly that the disparity of this genius with their present abilities did not at that time seem to occur to these flattered students. It is only fair to state, however, that most of these early disciples turned apostates to the faith and were not parties to the cult's later political designs.

Then in this private, secret document Saint Germain launched into a consideration of political and governmental matters, showing clearly the early desire of this "Ascended Master" for some sort of rulership over the kingdoms of earth, particularly that of America. We quote:

"All have come into this life with the desire to assist in perfecting or bringing into perfection that government of long ago into America at this time."

Some of these students, as stated, were or had been members of William Dudley Pelley's Silver Shirts of America. They were interested, therefore, in Saint Germain's statement that they would have a part in bringing the New Government into America—for had not Pelley himself been preaching the same thing to his disciples?

However, at the time that "Saint Germain" allegedly dictated this message, summer of 1934, Pelley was in difficulty with the courts of North Carolina. For months his publications were suppressed and the radio denied him. It appeared for a time that his strong nationally organized political movement might disintegrate.

Therefore, Saint Germain, astute politician that he was, addressed his remarks mainly to Pelley's sympathizers or dissenters in the group, with the intent no doubt of taking over the followers of this other movement.

"The first and essential thing to the perfection of that plan," he said, meaning the plan of his "New Government," "is being given." Then referring to Pelley's political order, he said:

"In *Christian Democracy* are splendid ideals possible of achievement." Later, referring to Pelley's economic textbook, he said:

"*The Plan of No More Hunger* is not entirely correct, but the *full plan* of it will be revealed as you move forward."

Having stated that Pelley's political order had "splendid ideals possible of achievement," he hints that there is a more "correct" plan—his own of course.

In this document Saint Germain refers also to other economic orders which followed the depression of 1929, mentioning the *Utopian Society of America, Plenocracy,* the *Paul Revere* activity, and suggests that some of these other movements could also be brought into "harmonious concord" with his own activity.

In fact, this adept at building upon the work of others, was astute enough to make the originator of Plenocracy his own personal "Messenger," subject, of course, to the orders of the Ballards!

"In Plenocracy," he says, "are splendid ideals." Then he goes on to indicate how "other ideas"—his own of course—could be blended into it. Artfully, he tells his "Friends of Long Ago":

"Neither Christian Democracy nor Plenocracy are perfect within themselves, but each has within it that upon which a *foundation* can be built.

"I think it would be much wiser for those knowing Mr. Pelley to work from the standpoint of Christian Democracy, and then as it can be done, *other ideas* be blended into it until the harmonious way of life can be presented to them. . . .

"Mr. Pelley was unprepared when the awakening came. Hence, it has made the activity very difficult, but if in all, or as rapidly as possible, the attention can be drawn to the constructive activity, I feel that very great good can come from it. . . .

"*Unveiled Mysteries* and *The Magic Presence* [the Ballard textbooks], with Mr. ————'s [naming Pelley's treasurer] activity in the knowledge of the Mighty I AM Presence, *will harmonize and prepare the Pelley group*. . . .

"It would not be wise for Mr. Pelley to have the discourses verbatim, unless sometime he wishes to come and receive them as the other students have done."

Thus did "Saint Germain" endeavor at that time to take over the followers of another movement. The plan, too, was to interest the Chief of the Silver Shirts in their "Saint Germain" and in their newly published book, and they wanted him to come to Chicago to get the instruction direct.

Indeed, Pelley's interest went so far that while in Chicago he had a visit with the Ballards.

But why should the Chief of the Silver Legionnaires, so accustomed to giving his own orders and contacting his own "Masters," play second fiddle and take orders from Saint Germain's three and only "Accredited Messengers," the two Ballards and their 16-year-old son Donald?

So Pelley declined Saint Germain's kind thought of having him study under the Ballards, and the Chief of the Silver Shirts has been without the questionable protection of this "Ascended Master" ever since.

However, even though the Ballards were unsuccessful in winning over the Chief himself, they won over Pelley's treasurer and right-hand man. They played for him as an angler does a prized catch, and when he went to Chicago, they clinched the matter by having Saint Germain make him nothing less than *"The Associate Director of the Saint Germain Activities!"*

Additionally showing the Silver Shirt background of the Ballard cult, we quote the following unsolicited letter from the Pelley Publishers, Asheville, N. C. It is dated January 10, 1938.

"It might interest you to know that Mrs. Ballard was a student of Mr. Pelley's spiritual philosophy before she launched upon her purported mission to "save" Christian America. All her writings and teachings are full of material which she appropriated from Mr. Pelley's writings."

Edna Ballard's interest in the Pelley movement extended over a period of years. At certain secret classes in Chicago, which she started in 1930, she read from Pelley's scripts and other "New Liberation" literature. During 1930-1932 she was laying the foundation for her own movement, with her husband then only taking a secondary part. In 1932 the two of them blossomed forth with the "Light and Sound Ray" idea; and in 1934, shortly after this secret ten-day class, they left Chicago to launch their national movement, gathering recruits for their "Save America" program largely among disillusioned Pelleyites.

CHAPTER 4

THE BALLARD SHOW GOES ON THE ROAD

In this first ten-day class held at Chicago in the summer of 1934 was a man who innocently, it seems, became the victim of the Ballard strategy. This man was one of William Dudley Pelley's faithful workers, whom we mentioned in the last chapter, a prominent Silver Shirter and treasurer of the organization. He had read the Ballard book, *Unveiled Mysteries*, then just out, and, after some correspondence with its author, went to Chicago to attend this first ten-day class.

Here was an opportunity for the financially embarrassed Ballards to really start their movement and get out of their economic doldrums. This man's wide experience with the Pelley organization could be used, and his contact with key Legionnaires throughout the country would be just what they needed to promote their own religio-patriotic movement. So they did what they could to swing him their way.

No doubt the former Pelleyite was influenced into sincerely believing the Ballards had something to give the world. He had battled hard for Pelley in the court action against him in Asheville, N. C., and now he was discouraged and somewhat disillusioned as well. The Ballard metaphysics seemed a heaven compared to what he had gone through in fighting Pelley's political battles. The two metaphysical systems were very similar, but the ideality and beautiful summerland of ease and plenty pictured by the Ballards in their book intrigued him as nothing else ever had.

Were not the never-failing *Ascended Masters* in charge of the new order and *not* a storm-centered Pelley? They in their divine power and wisdom would bring in the new Republic. They would bring a heaven on earth. They would emancipate humanity from the three thieves—disease, poverty, and death. It would all happen in perfect divine order, without revolution, court actions, militant Legionnaires, racial hatreds, brown shirts, white shirts, silver shirts, or any of the storm-troop trappings of a world besieged by human leaders dominated by fascistic desires and principles.

All this and much more, in effect, had been stated in that marvelous new book for the New Age—*Unveiled Mysteries*. Lawyers, doctors, clergymen, and even hardheaded business men had read it, and, after looking over the topsy-turvy world, were persuaded in spite of themselves to believe it. So was Pelley's treasurer. Was it not a way out of all the mess?

The "Accredited Messengers of the Ascended Masters" lost no time in their efforts to crystallize these thoughts. In a letter to Pelley's treasurer dated September 6, 1934, written and signed in pen and ink by Guy Ballard himself, the senior messenger says:

"Blessed Brother, I have no right to say this, but I know it is right to cut yourself completely loose from Pelley in every way."

The outcome of the matter was that Pelley's trusted employe became the "*Associate Director of the Saint Germain Activities.*" For three months he promoted the Ballards on the lecture platform in the east until an automobile accident, which happened when he stepped out of the Ballard car, cut short his usefulness to "Saint Germain" and his Messengers.

Pelley in a special bulletin to his people describing his difficulties with the courts of North Carolina, which he graphically entitled "*The Battle of Asheville,*" commented on the defection of his former supporter in this wise:

"One real shadow cast over the proceedings was the word received on the fourth day of the trial that our former Treasurer, ————————————, who had quit the Silver Shirt work . . . . called Liberation people together to sell them instead on the work of the Ballard-King Group in Chicago, had suddenly met with a terrible auto accident in Baltimore and been rushed to the Johns Hopkins Hospital with a fractured skull and compound fracture of the left leg."

"*Strange, strange indeed*," very meaningly commented the Silver Shirt chief, "*are the denouement of events in the lives of those who take up the Silvershirt work and then turn back.*" And then he goes on to recount the misfortunes of other workers who had deserted the cause.

Again the parallelism between the two movements, and their methods of holding their people, is inescapable. But the Ballards and their "Masters," as we shall find, have gone much further than Pelley in putting the fear of disaster into the minds of those who "*turn back.*"

As might be expected, considering this former treasurers's influence among the Pelleyites, the first "I AM" audiences were recruited largely from members of the Silver Shirt organization. And so the Saint Germain "Mighty I AM" movement got well under way right from the start. "Saint Germain" had started to build his movement on the foundation of another one, just as he had planned.

Through the efforts of this former Silver Shirter the first out-of-town class was held in Philadelphia during the early part of October, 1934. The Ballards chose not to use their real names, for reasons which will later be clear, and so they were introduced as *Mr. and Mrs. Godfre Ray King,* "*Accredited Messengers of the Ascended Master Saint Germain.*"

This was the real start of the movement, although the

foundation for it had been made in 1932, and even a year
or two before when Edna Ballard was holding secret classes
while her husband was "traveling in the Far East," or for
other reasons (to be discovered) only occasionally showing
up at the classes.

From 1934 on, beginning at Philadelphia, the Mighty
I AM movement began to take hold of the imagination
and fancy of metaphysical and patriotic people. Starting
with thirty persons the first night, the attendance grew
until toward the end of the ten days a hundred and fifty
were in attendance.

People *wanted* the things that Mr. and Mrs. Godfre
Ray King so authoritatively promised, and they were willing to pay for them. At the close of the class the Ballards
and their Associate Director divided $300.00 between
them as clear profit.

It was sadly needed, for despite the enormous stores of
gold assertedly held by Saint Germain in his private retreat
in the mountain, the Ballards were in most straightened
financial circumstances. They made no secret of the fact
that they even used their rent money due on their modest
Chicago bungalow to pay their railroad fare to Philadelphia
to start their movement.

Saint Germain with his discourses was most liberal,
but with his gold he was most penurious. Despite the
fact that he assertedly had gold nuggets, coins, and "Spanish gold lost at sea," all neatly stored away in a secret
retreat in the mountain, his own Accredited Messengers
had to beg, borrow, and bargain to get out this "Ascended
Master" gentleman's own books. Not one cent of it came
from the stored wealth of this modern Croesus. It came
from the pocketbooks of the "Beloved Students" in dimes
and dollars and gold, for the audiences were requested in
the early days not to put copper pennies into the collection
plate. *Gold* and not copper was to be the symbol and
god of this cult.

From Philadelphia the Godfre Ray Kings went to New York, then to Boston. In both places they stirred the psychic waters to some degree with their claims and promises. By the time these lectures were over, the expectant students in Philadelphia were clamoring for more "Ascended Master Miracles." These miracles, of course, were only on paper, as it were, but they were accepted by the Beloved Ones on a sort of psychic promissory note.

So a return engagement was staged in the City of Brotherly Love, with similar successes for the Ray Kings, but without the promised miracles for the Beloved Students.

And before a month was scarcely up, the hurrying New Yorkers were calling for another ten-day class. This Saint Germain graciously agreed to, but again it was without benefit of miracles.

The great Mighty I AM movement was now well under way, both financially and metaphysically speaking. But in those early days it was only a dim shadow of its coming grandeur, only a side show compared to the later five-ring performance which swept on from city to city luring the unsuspecting with psychic pink lemonade and other sure-fire circus ballyhoo.

Like most road shows the Ballard extravaganza followed in the wake of the seasons. In the winter it was found in sunny California or Florida, with, however, the Golden State winning out most of the time. In the spring and fall it traveled to favored eastern cities. In the hot summer months it lingered near the cool breezes of the Pacific. "Saint Germain," the director of the show and the one responsible for its itinerary, has always been most sensitive to the physical comforts of his Messengers.

Fresh from these early successes on the Eastern Coast, the two Kings and their son Donald moved southward, stopping over for a ten-day class at our Nation's capital during the early part of January, 1935.

It must have been with strange feelings of personal possession that the Ballards parked their newly acquired Ford car in political Washington. Here, allegedly, was the scene of the political labors of their mysterious Comte de St. Germain in his endeavors to bring about his "New Government" in America. He had promised his "Friends of Long Ago"—the growing "I AM" family—they would have a part in it. And surely his own "Accredited Messengers," would not exactly be forgotten in the new dispensation.

Indeed, Guy Ballard, so we are informed, had held a very high office during a former incarnation in this very city of Washington, and had a name to which all Americans, including little school children, pay special reverence on stated occasions. We shall a little later tell all about this.

So here was Ballard, his wife and son again back in the city of his past achievements. And right at his elbow, to lead him to victory over the "vicious forces anchored in Washington," was the mighty Saint Germain and a whole legion of "Ascended Masters."

After this little sojourn at the American capital, Ballard and his family moved on for further fields to conquer, but left a promise to return to this center of the Nation's life with more power of the "Light Rays" than before.

Their design was to take in the solid South and bring it under "Ascended Master" domination. But Circumstance is ever the maker and breaker of empire, and their day was not exactly to break with full glory in the South.

The tragic accident to their Associate Director, which occurred on the night of their last lecture in Washington, intervened to check their fast-building Ascended Master empire.

As this man stepped out of the Ballard car, he was hit by a fast-moving automobile which came tearing along in the early morning hours of January 13, 1935, and this faithful servant of the Ballards, one whom Saint Germain frequently called his "pal," lay maimed and apparently dying in the roadway.

For months he was totally incapacitated for any further use either to Saint Germain, who had promised faithfully to protect him from any harm, or to the Ballards who had guaranteed him the protection of the entire Cosmic Host. However, apparently not having any faith in their own powers of healing or those of their Master, they wired a physical-plane mental healer in a nearby state for help, and left their friend and Assoicate Director in a critical condition in the hands of the surgeons at Johns Hopkins Hospital in Baltimore.

With recovery came gradual disillusionment for this man. He wrote us in 1936, shortly after we had published the first brochure exposing some of the hoax of this cult. We are indebted to him for supplying documents and information concerning the early beginnings of this movement. Below are a few excerpts from his correspondence at that time:

"You may be interested in knowing that I am the poor *Sap* who found the Ballards stranded out in Chicago, and thinking they really had something that would benefit humanity, I took them out and started them on their mad conquest.

"I took them to Philadelphia, New York, Boston, and Washington; and after finishing at Washington and leaving there, I was hit by an auto, thrown a hundred feet and then run over. I was terribly mangled, my head being terribly fractured and my left leg broken . . .

"I was driving their car. . . . They gave out that my accident happened because I wasn't in the circle of Light with which they had surrounded the car; yet, later on, in St. Petersburg while Ballard, with Don driving, was in the car, they had an accident. The car was so demolished they had to get a new car and Ballard couldn't finish the classes. I was told he had a rib or two broken. . . .

"I surely should like to see them stopped from their lying and deceiving. . . . They told it here in Philadelphia that the real ——————— [naming himself] died in the hospital

and the present ——————— [himself] now walking
around is another entity occupying this body!

"I had no business to tie up with such people. It is a
terrible thing to me and has preyed terribly on my mind
and my soul for releasing and starting the terrible thing
which they represent."

After the accident to this man, the three divinely-
appointed Messengers turned their Ford car southward
and continued doubtlessly in a none-too-happy frame of
mind toward the sunny climes of Florida. They passed
through Richmond during a blinding snowstorm with
Mrs. Ballard fighting a throat cold which she had acquired
during the two closing days of the Washington class.

At last they reached West Palm Beach for their scheduled ten-day class, but the South was not so easily taken
in as the North, financially or metaphysically, causing Mr.
Ballard to write: *"The Love Gifts were less in West Palm
Beach than usual."*

It was in Miami, however, that the Messengers met
with the most provoking circumstances. The Ballard contact-man there, a former Silver Shirter, was delegated to
make the arrangements for the usual ten-day class, hire
a good hall, and do the other things which good lecturers
like to have well done.

But the hall selected was not very satisfactory. In
fact, Mr. Ballard wrote to a friend on February 7th in
his own handwriting saying: *"The hall he got here isn't
fit for a dog fight, let alone an Ascended Master Activity."*

It seems that Saint Germain, who attends so well to
more important matters, not only let his own Messengers
down in the matter of a lecture hall, but other matters as
well, for on March 13th Messenger Ballard, who promises
his students absolute mastery over circumstances, wrote:
*"You will never know the forces we have been pitted
against since we left Washington."*

What some of these "forces" were will now be told.

It appears the Ballard contact-man in Miami had come to the conclusion that despite the Accredited Messengers' claims and vaunted power over circumstances, they were just like other ordinary people—subject to little provoking happenings as well as to tragic events. He found that Mrs. Ballard was suffering from a cold, that daddy Ballard had a temper when things didn't go right, that son Donald could use on occasions un-Ascended Master invectives, that their Associate Director had just had a tragic automobile accident in the service of the Ascended Masters, and that Saint Germain himself was conspicuous by his continued and unexplained absence at the hall and elsewhere.

He forthwith decided that the whole thing was a hoax and concluded he might as well play this little game of "Saint Germain" himself. So one night he got down to the hall early before the crowds had arrived, padlocked the door and put a sign on it reading:

"CLOSED BY ORDER OF SAINT GERMAIN!"

Mr. Ballard in describing this tragic little incident in a letter dated February 12, said:

"He is a fiend, the most vicious I have met, and don't anybody try to tell me he is not. On the door in typewriting, read, 'Closed by Saint Germain's Order,' showing he was trying to assume *my* Authority with Saint Germain. That is *Insanity*."

We learn here that instead of Saint Germain having authority over his own messenger, Messenger Ballard has authority over his own Master—a queer reversal of the time-honored relationship, giving the suspicion that the high and mighty Saint Germain is nothing more than Ballard's man Friday.

Such incidents as related were but some of the forces against which Ballard said they had been pitted since leaving Washington, as we shall see, proving that "Whom the Ascended Master loveth he chasteneth."

Under the instruction of Saint Germain himself, they were told to arrange classes at St. Petersburg, but as this all-knowing Ascended Master from the Seventh Octave of Light did not know that this saintly old city exacts a $500 lecture fee for itinerant lecturers, which was not forthcoming from his gold reserves at his secret mountain retreat, the idea of lecturing there wasn't exactly feasible even for Saint Germain's Accredited Messengers.

His Messengers, therefore, had to arrange for their class at Pass-a-Grille, a fishing town about twelve miles from St. Petersburg, which did not exact a cover charge to this feast of the Mighty I AM.

But here new tragedy struck out of the blue. Messenger Ballard had told the good Florida people about his marvelous protection, that nothing could hurt him, and the *Magic Presence* manuscript had told of his body of *"Immortal Endurance."* Mrs. Ballard was holding the fort at the lecture hall in Pass-a-Grille waiting for her husband and son to show up so that the meeting could begin. Minutes passed, then hours, and not even Saint Germain, who knows all the secret agreements of European diplomats and the sublime mysteries of the universe, divulged the news to the waiting audience that son Donald had driven their new Ford car into a ditch, and with it Saint Germain's own senior Messenger!

Donald, not having a body of immortal endurance, was uninjured, but Mr. Ballard's immortal body sustained a couple of broken ribs.

To the faithful such a thing will doubtless seem impossible, but we quote from Guy Ballard's letter written to a friend under date of April 2, 1935:

"Your beautiful letter received at Pass-a-Grille and I would have answered it from there but our car turned over and my ribs were fractured and I am just now catching up my correspondence."

These happenings, however, did not permanently

dampen the Ascended Master ardor of the Accredited
Messengers. The goal was westward toward the peaceful
Pacific, to the land of promise, Southern California, and
especially to that favored Los Angeles region which has
ever been the mecca for things metaphysical and unusual.

Saint Germain's advance agents, mostly disillusioned
Silver Shirters, had been contacted and everything was
ripe for the entry of the Accredited Messengers of Saint
Germain into the city of the Angels.

Glowing accounts of these marvelous people had been
spread among the metaphysical elect of Los Angeles, and
they in turn had passed the good news on to their students
and friends. No bill boards splashed the countryside, but
the telephonic wires were hot with the news of the near-
arrival of Comte de St. Germain's Accredited Messengers.

A few of the more prominent metaphysical leaders
and teachers were invited to meet the Messengers privately
at their hotel when they arrived. These private interviews
and first classes were largely successful because of the
enthusiastic acclaim for the Messengers by a man of promi-
nence in the occult field, both here and abroad, whom the
Ballards had been fortunate to secure as their new manager after the unfortunate accident of their former Associate Director.

At these private interviews and during the first classes
Mrs. Ballard dressed simply and unostentatiously. It was
not until the flood gates of wealth opened up in Los
Angeles through the book sales and love gifts of students
that this simplicity changed to the gorgeousness which
later has characterized her every appearance.

During these first interviews and classes she spoke with
seeming authority of her close contact with her beloved
Master. And while Mr. Ballard, meek and spiritual looking, let his more expressive wife do most of the direct selling, the far-away mystic look in his eyes spoke volumes.

This effective and characteristic teamwork put them

over with many of the metaphysical leaders, and, as a result, these Los Angeles teachers announced to their classes the arrival of the Accredited Messengers of Comte de St. Germain, *"Der Wundermann"* of 18th-century Europe. They urged their students to hear these marvelous people, and some even closed their classes to have their students attend *en masse*.

This gesture of friendliness and cooperation, however, was later regretted by many of these teachers. With chagrin and astonishment they heard Count St. Germain's Messengers proclaim to their own hard-earned students that the *"old occult order had been set aside,"* had become obsolete and even dangerous, and thenceforth, the *"Saint Germain"* teachings, as put out *only* by Mr. and Mrs. G. W. Ballard and son Donald, would have charge over the occult destinies of mankind!

The result was a sudden and disastrous swing of metaphysical students to the new leadership and the old was left out very much in the metaphysical cold.

All is fair, it seems, in love and war and with the Mighty I AM of the Ballards, tending to prove at least superficially that the end justifies the means among occult dictators as well as among the political variety.

CHAPTER 5

THE RISE OF A DICTATOR

During the spring and summer of 1935, while yet in California, the Ballard metaphysical machine made good progress, as was to be expected in a land where the milk and honey of strange doctrines flows so freely. From the early and more simple presentation of the Saint Germain teachings the movement gradually took the form of a complicated ritualism, wherein decrees and taboos were rigorously enunciated by a feminine dictator.

At first this authoritative control over the lives of its members was not so apparent. The individual students and class leaders were allowed a certain freedom of thought and action, but this personal liberty the leaders no doubt found to be a weakness which worked against their long cherished personal ambitions.

Perhaps, too, a certain incident, which will now be related, brought strongly to their attention the need for central control over their rising kingdom of "I AM" worshippers. Then again, doubtless, they had in mind the "New Government" Saint Germain had promised to set up in his beloved America with an "Ascended Master" on the throne at the White House. All this of course would require central control and *dictatorship*, not individual freedom.

Expanding audiences in Los Angeles necessitated the Ballards on three successive occasions to seek larger halls, until "Saint Germain" decided that the large Shrine Civic Auditorium, seating over six thousand persons, was the place for his prospering Messengers who at last were coming into their own. A ten-day class was scheduled there in

August of 1935, which closed in what was designated as "a blaze of glory." Since then, this auditorium which has been headquarters for great national conventions of Shriners, has also been "Convention Headquarters" for I AM-ers, attracting the faithful in large numbers at least twice a year from all parts of the country.

This "Shrine" meeting was the eighth large class held on the Pacific Coast during the Ballards' first surprising circuit. They had lectured also in San Francisco, Seattle, Pasadena, Long Beach, San Diego, and were flushed with victory, money, and Messianic fervor. Then their show moved eastward for engagements in Kansas City, New York, Boston, Philadelphia, and Washington.

It is interesting to note that these two people and their son Donald arrived in Los Angeles in a none-too-prosperous condition in an unpretentious car, but when they left, they zoomed away in a couple of flashy cream-colored Chryslers. Following in their wake were a number of the beloved students, seeking through a sort of psychic induction process to partake of the radiance of the "Ascended Masters."

While the Messengers were absent, the work on the Pacific coast was to be organized by a gentleman whom Saint Germain appointed as head of a "Sevenfold Committee." But despite the fact that these seven individuals had been personally selected and approved by the un-erring Saint Germain himself, there was much dissension and argument among the members of this committee as to how the work should be carried on during the Messengers' absence. It seems that Saint Germain himself was not very certain just how it should be done.

The mushroom growth of numerous "I AM Classes" and the sudden ascension into power of many leaders— each a little uncertain what the "I AM" was all about— and each no doubt with certain personal ambitions of his own, brought on a condition of Ascended Master affairs which the decrees of the students could not correct nor the imagined presence of the great "Saint Germain" straighten out.

It seemed for a while as if the whole movement on the Pacific Coast was due to go up in smoke from so much friction of personal dissension among the members of the divinely appointed "Sevenfold Committee."

Then it was that Edna Ballard displayed her, as yet, untried capacity for autocratic leadership and domination over her "I AM" family. Dispatching one of her characteristic "Saint Germain-signed letters" to the head of the Sevenfold Committee, this surprised gentleman was summarily dismissed without a hearing and the whole cosmically-approved septenary forthwith dissolved.

Suspicious, too, that their own manager, who was then with them in the east, had gotten under the influence of another teaching and was somehow involved in the disturbed Los Angeles happenings, another "Saint Germain letter" was handed to this gentleman which caused him to resign as their *second* officially-appointed "Associate Director."

Then cancelling some of their eastern engagements, the Ballards hastened to the scene of the Los Angeles dissension to straighten out a condition which Saint Germain could not handle from the psychic plane—or, as the credulous believe—from the Ascended Masters' "*Seventh Octave of Light.*"

Appearing more or less unexpectedly at a meeting of prominent students and class leaders at the Sindelar Studios, the two Ballards electrified their audience by the power and authority with which they assertedly spoke.

Edna in particular rose to the heights of a feminine dictator. In characteristic pose and eloquence she flayed the discharged head of Saint Germain's "Sevenfold Committee," impugning him of base motives, and by threat and intimidation warned those within reach of her voice what terrible things would happen if they did not follow the instruction of the Ascended Masters as given by their three and only "Accredited Messengers."

"The great Law " she said, "would no longer protect those who were disobedient, and any violation would be quickly punished—and be felt in the next two or three embodiments."

She caused the distribution of the two assertedly dictated "Saint Germain letters" among the class leaders to be read to their students at their classes to further show that the Ascended Masters really meant business.

The letter sent through the U. S. Mails to the head of the Sevenfold Committee in Los Angeles is reproduced here in its entirety, with the exception that all personal names are left out.

"*Saint Germain*" is responsible for the grammatical construction, misspelled, and misused words.

Washington, D. C.
November 26, 1935

_____

You are now dismissed from any further privilege or authority to serve the Messengers, Myself, or any other of the Ascended Masters in this embodiment.

To willingly try to deceive earnest students seeking their freedom in the Light is unpardonable. You have made yourself a claw of the sinister force in coming into the association ——————— [naming two leaders of two other movements]. My pity goes out to you and——————— [naming their own manager], for your complete freedom for both of you was at hand when the Messengers were in Long Beach. There was so much good in both of you and now to allow it to be so distorted as has been done. Too late will you cry out in agony for the mistake you have made.

Your earth span is very short. Make peace with your God and call on the Law of Forgiveness while there is yet time, less you deprive yourself of opportunity in the next embodiment. Do not try to bluff such deception through any longer, less you do this thing again in the next two embodiments.

When you willingly put yourself under the red Light,

you cut off the White Light.

My Love and hope goes out to you, that you may yet face about and calling on the Law of Forgiveness, call sufficient assistance to cut you free of this sinister claw.

I AM making this one last attempt to help you. *Choose.* The All-seeing Eye of God is upon you.

SAINT GERMAIN.

This interesting little "Ascended Master" document was sent from their hotel in Washington, D. C., with the Ballard name on the envelope. No doubt the fact of their being in the National Capital, which was Saint Germain's field of political operations in his efforts to bring about his "New Government," gave these people an added sense of dictatorial power—and a legal protection from sending a threatening letter through the mails.

Just two months before, the Ballards had written this same gentleman that for his wonderful service to the "Light," he would be *"forever* blessed," and that they and "Saint Germain" knew the "motive in his heart" was as "pure and true as a diamond."

This later letter from "Saint Germain," with its threat, *"Your earth span is very short,"* was surely not intended to *"bless"* this gentleman quite *"forever."* Neither was the additional threat, *"Too late will you cry out in agony,"* intended to be a helpful morning thought.

The I AM-er's god known as "Saint Germain" is a revengeful god, visiting his wrath upon his errant ones not only in this present embodiment but even unto, as he says in his letter, the *"next two embodiments!"*

The prophecy—if such it can be called—of this gentleman's early death was made over four years ago, but unfortunately for Saint Germain's prowess as a soothsayer, the gentleman in question is still very much alive.

The effect of these threats, however, on the general mass of followers, was all that could be desired. The scattered group leaders, some of whom had been teaching unauthorized doctrines not countenanced by the Accredited Messengers or who had otherwise been disobedient, were so impressed by the power and authority of the Ascended Masters as displayed by Edna Ballard and the Saint Germain letter that they very readily acquiesed to this assumption of divine authority. Indeed most of them feared to do otherwise, and were glad to have this new papal protection from all the terrible things that would happen to those who disobeyed.

Very few troubled themselves about really finding out what crime these two individuals had committed to deserve such Ascended Master wrath. It seems that they had merely been guilty of doing a little thinking of their own, and along with this forbidden sin they had presumed to show some interest in a similar teaching. Such a thing, of course, was not to be countenanced in a dictatorship. In addition to this, the Ballards seized upon their "sin" as an opportunity to make them the goats, as it were, of this Los Angeles upheaval—an occasion for the dictators to demonstrate a new and more dominant assertion of their papal power.

The "humble Messengers" of Saint Germain made the most of their opportunity, and since that early crisis in California their control has become more and more dominant and their movement increasingly autocratic, intolerant, belligerant, and tyrannical.

Thus Guy and Edna Ballard's long cherished ambitions for gold and power were at last about to be realized, even though they had sometimes to ride roughshod over those who had faithfully served them. A dictator cannot be squeamish about friendship, particularly when that friendship does not subserve certain ends. And so through this Los Angeles incident Edna Lotus Ray King Ballard, Priestess of the Mighty I AM movement, rose to new heights of dictatorship and achieved in part her long cherished ambition to be ruler over the lives of many.

CHAPTER 6

PSYCHOLOGICAL BUGABOOS

In the good old horse and buggy days, before more modern methods of teaching children were in vogue, the favorite pastime of some parents for making their rambunctious youngsters obey was to scare them into thinking the *"bugaboo man"* would get them if they "didn't watch out."

Just who and where the bugaboo man was nobody would tell, and that made the subject even more dark and mysterious. But nevertheless it was all very real to little country children who were sent to bed in dimly lighted rooms where an old lamp or a tallow candle cast strange and eerie shadows on the walls.

Now, in a very real sense, the Ballard psychology has played upon such primitive fears of the human race—fears that came in the childhood of the race which civilized people take for granted they have long since outgrown. To perpetrate such bugaboo stories on grown-up intelligent people in an era of incandescent light seems the height of absurdity and unreality, yet that is the exact psychology which lies back of the Ballard control over their people. It shows to what extent childlike credulity and fear are still governing factors in lives of people today.

In the Ballard system, the bugaboo man masquerades under many different guises. Sometimes, he is of seeming high character, even an "Ascended Master," who, despite his professed love for his "beloved children," will scare them into unquestioning and abject obedience. At other times the Ballard bogey is really bad—an evil "astral entity," or, worse, a "black magician," who will cast a spell over his victim or take possession of his body if he doesn't watch out. Between these two types of bogey-men the "I AM" student is caught, and is made to obey—or else.

It is this psychological domination of unseen "Masters" and imaginary bogeys upon the minds of superstitious people that holds so many to the Ballard cult. Like the Trojan horse of the Spartans, these ideas have been placed within the gates of the citadel of the mind, and when reason slumbers, they issue forth to do their mischief.

So long as the Ballards can keep their psychologized students believing that Saint Germain is a great "Cosmic Being," and not their "man Friday," they can no doubt maintain their weird dictatorship. But once their students begin to lose faith in their invisible hierarchy of "Ascended Masters," they will see the "Accredited Messengers" as they really are, and will throw the Trojan horse and all its mischief makers from out the high citadel of the mind.

It is this psychological danger which so greatly permeates the Ballard movement. Its leaders seek in every possible way to keep students from thinking for themselves. They try constantly to prevent their people from reading anything that seeks to tell the truth about their movement. They inject into the minds of their students thoughts of terrible consequences that will result should they dare criticize or question one little thing concerning this "Ascended Master" instruction.

When the author published his first analytical brochure on the absurdities of this movement back in 1936, entitled: *The "I AM" Experiences of Mr. G. W. Ballard*, the collective Ballard wrath knew no end, and students were urged to burn every copy they could get their hands on—but without reading it first.

Some of the more fanatical ones literally carried these instructions out. They rushed down to book stores and bought these books with good American money; and then

book burning

to show their faithfulness to the Ballards and the approving "Ascended Masters," they consigned the collection to ashes. They conducted book-burning parties, and with proper ceremonies these "terrible books" were burned with all the fanaticism of a witch-burning rite, reminiscent of a former age of bigotry and superstition.

These book-burning parties, however, unfortunately for the author, did not continue. Saner moments—or perhaps the Scotch in some of the students—told them that this kind of thing would be too expensive to continue, and that so long as Saint Germain permitted the printing presses to run, these books would appear. So the bonfires were discontinued for lack of fuel and at a saving of the pocketbook, and the presence of these books which had brought so much fear to the leaders had to be accepted in the same way as the students accept the existence of astral entities and black magicians. However, like good warriors, they still do battle against such things.

"Saint Germain," as might be expected, was particularly incensed about any form of criticism—particularly when he was the object and *not* the dispenser of it, and he developed a well-defined persecution complex, imagining certain organizations were "spying" on him or his work.

" . . . Every source," says the irate Saint Germain, "whether it is Unity, Christian Science or whatever it is, that attempts to bring disgrace upon This Work or condemns or criticizes It, will fail utterly and their churches will be empty!" (p. 55, A.M.D.)

Some months later, the long-haired "Tall Master from Venus" took up Saint Germain's fight against organizations, but as the memory of this Venusian "Master" is as short as that of earth mortals, he forgot which one of his numerous "Ascended Master" brethren made the above prediction, and erroneously stated:

"The *Great Divine Director* [!] said many months ago that if the Christian Scientists did not stop opposing

this work they would empty their churches; if the orthodox world did not stop it they would empty their churches.
Well my dear ones, if I were to tell you, tonight, how
many churches have already been emptied and closed you
would be astonished. (p. 25, Oct., 1938, v.)

We hope that the information given by the Tall Master
from Venus concerning the "emptying of the churches"
is as faulty as his memory.

For the benefit of those who are uninformed as to the
manner in which the numerous Ballard "Masters" contact
this earth plane of ours, we will say that it is all done
through the vocal cords of their senior Messenger. Guy
Ballard appears on the platform and informs the audience
that the "God Himalaya," or some other great "Ascended
Master" would that day have the dictation. Then, just as
easy as you please, Ballard repeats the discourse which is
flashed to him, he says, in "living letters of Light," while
the "blessed ones" in the audience try their best to see this
great "Master" and his flaming letters.

Some, quite naturally and inevitably, hypnotize themselves into doing this rather well. The easily observable
fact that *all* of these numerous "Gods," "Masters," and
even fair "Goddesses" say the same things, use the same
phraseology, slang, and idiom, doesn't seem to reveal the
fake to these trusting, heaven-bent souls.

Quite often, too, Guy Ballard, at the receiving end of
the line, is a little forgetful. Unconsciously, in the midst
of his "Ascended Master" discourse, he sometimes takes
out his watch to see how much longer the "Ascended
Master" has to talk, quite forgetting that the great and
all-wise Being who is *supposed* to be talking should know
what time it was himself!

Catching himself one day in the act of taking out his
watch, while none other than the great "Cosmic Master
Ray-O-Light" was delivering the discourse, he had that
great Being lamely apologize for his absent-mindedness by

saying: " . . . Seeing the Messenger look at his watch, I take it for granted that he is still recognizing time and space. Perhaps in this instance, it is quite justifiable." (p. 19, Oct., 1939, v.) With all of which we are inclined to agree.

While this may either be amusing or disgusting to the *unbeliever* in such nonsense, to the poor student it is all mighty serious business. These students *fear* the terrible power which the "Accredited Messengers" and their "Masters" assertedly wield. Many fear to talk to, or have anything to do with, former members of the movement who were once their most cherished friends. Such are ostracized and condemned as "vicious" because they have had the courage to withdraw from the movement. Cowed and even terrified, some fear to withdraw even though they have more than a suspicion that all is not gold that glitters in this "Light-of-God-that-Never-Fails" movement.

Early in the work, Saint Germain, *through the Ballards*, appointed eight "Messengers" who were to take orders from the three and only "Accredited" Messengers. Six of the eight, for various and sundry misdemeanors, have all been fired or have voluntarily withdrawn from the movement.

When some one of these messengers or other prominent member was to be fired, Saint Germain was usually called in from weighty European problems to officiate in that capacity. A little diversion which he no doubt accepted with his usual grace.

In 1937 one of the eight original messengers had incurred the divine displeasure and was to be fired. In due time he received one of the characteristic "Saint Germain letters" written on Edna Ballard's little typewriter.

This man's wife, who also was numbered among the original eight, was not guilty of any crime against the holy set-up, but nevertheless she was fired at the same time because she *just happened to be his wife!* A sort of vicarious criminality, as it were.

Saint Germain's (?) letter is herewith reproduced in part. It was sent from a Philadelphia hotel, where the Ballards were staying, and signed "SAINT GERMAIN"—on the typewriter. The spelling, punctuation, etc., is that of its creator.

May 18, 1937,
11 A. M.

Mr. ———
Mrs. ———

Owing to your continued spreading of vicious falsehood, concerning My Work and the Magnificent Dictations of Discourses by many of the Ascended Masters, your compel Me to withdraw your Messengership, which I gave you represent Me and My Work.

It is unfortunate that Mrs. ——— [this man's wife] must be included in this, as her Light is bright and her heart is right; but being associated with you, I am compelled to withdraw the Messengership from her, also.

If you could realize your great mistake in this attitude to My Work, you could call on the Law of Forgiveness and thus avoid the conditions you must meet in your next embodiment . . .

You have built up a vicious hate entity that is surely destroying you . . . You shall not any longer represent Me, or have privilege of selling the books . . . This you have brought upon yourself . . .

May your Mighty I AM Presence release you from the tragic danger you are in.

SAINT GERMAIN

This document with its threats of "tragic danger" and "destroying entities," even unto this poor man's "next embodiment," would have been more convincing if it had been written in Saint Germain's own "beautiful script" (see page 73, U. M.) and had been stamped with the grand seal of Saint Germain's secret retreat in the Wyoming mountains. But, no, it evidently came fresh and hot, and none too accurate, from Mrs. Ballard's typewriter at their hotel room in the City of Brotherly Love.

CHAPTER 7

THE WAR ON "ENTITIES"

A week or so hobnobbing among the Ballard followers at their "I AM Temples" is usually enough to convince the visitor that a gigantic warfare is being waged between the decreeing I AM-er and his "entities."

We must here explain that by "entities" is meant the teeming horde of "psychic" creations that are supposed to populate the world around us, of which, most fortunately, the average person is unaware until certain teachings and practices begin to make such people "entity conscious." The Ballard cult has done much to bring on well-developed cases of psychophobia in otherwise normal people.

Everywhere, it seems, there are entities. They peep out at I AM-ers from every antique. They nestle in the auras of people who oppose their movement. They bump their heads against protective "walls of Light" thrown around the faithful students. They are as numerous as a plague of locusts, and highly suggestible students are constantly doing battle against them.

Thousands of dollars worth of valuable antiques have been burned or otherwise destroyed by fanatical students because they were told by the Ballards that such things always swarm with entities.

Until the Ballards came along, these possessions were most harmless. But with the advent of the Accredited Messengers of Saint German, they suddenly became alive with haunting spirits of the dead.

The Ballards have a "decree," supposed to take care of the matter, and the students go around shouting it at any suspicious thing or person that appears to harbor an entity.

But these "entities" are persistent little imps. They scurry for cover when an irate I AM-er gets after them, and appear to sneak right back again when the coast is clear.

And so despite their decrees and other safeguards, the undeclared war on entities in America still continues, and the outcome of the matter is as yet quite uncertain. So much so that the primordial battle between the dog and his fleas has nothing on the battle which rages between the average I AM-er and his latest crop of entities.

The technique of giving an "Entity Decree" for a well-directed blitzkrieg against the enemy seems to be about as follows:

First, the student calls on the "Mighty I AM Presence," and, usually, some one or more of the "Ascended Masters." Most of them always manage to include the "Blessed Saint Germain," as, under all circumstances, he is a most potent protection. But for absolute safety, they include some of the others, at least a "Goddess" or two, or one of the "Lords of the Flame" from Venus.

"*Oromasis*" is a favorite with some of the students, but latterly it appears that "*Mighty Astrea*" is a close runner-up for favor among really discriminating I AM-ers.

After selection of suitable gods and goddesses has been duly accomplished, the student raises his or her hands heavenward and vehemently commands these "Mighty Beings" from the "Seventh Octave of Light" to—

"Send Legions of Thy Angel Devas of the Blue Lightning of Divine Love to seize, bind, and remove from within and around me and my world all entities—carnate and discarnate—forever! If they be of human creation, *annihilate* them, their cause and effect this instant. If they be discarnate, take them out of the atmosphere of earth . . . " etc.

I AM-ers, when they want quick action over some

entity or other evil, frequently use the words *"Blast! Blast! Blast!"*

For instance, one stopped with her companion in front of a downtown shop window. On display was a black gown with red trimmings! These are hated colors among the I AM-ers—the color of the black magician and the communist! All she did was to stop at the window for a second, looked at the gown; then, to the amazement of her companion, uttered very vehemently the words *"Blast! Blast! Blast!"* in an aspirate voice, and passed on, evidently feeling a duty had been performed.

The ancient Babylonians, it seems, had similar methods of dealing with the "entity" situation in those dark days.

Compare the following Babylonian decree with the Ballard one. It is a translation from cuneiform writing on ancient Babylonian clay tablets, copied from a book at the Los Angeles Public Library, and is addressed to the Babylonian god "Gilgamesh"—almost as odd a name as the Ballard god "Oromasis." We quote:

"Gilgamesh, thou Mighty of the Mighty! Lord of the Red Flames, Lord of the Blue Flames, of the clouds and darkness.

"Hear, O Mighty One, Let thy Thunder descend and *Blast the Spirits* that haunt my pathway!

"Amen, Lord of the Golden Light, King beyond all Kings.

"Command thy Messengers of the Yellow Flame to *consume* and *destroy* all obstacles that mock me!

"Hear, I command!"

We find ourselves wondering what it was that destroyed Babylon, and wonder at the forces of evil playing through the modern Babylon of today.

But out of all this warfare upon entities has emerged a Cosmic hero, a generalissimo, who has been assigned to clean up the entity slums of the nation—and right royally has he done it!

His name is "*Mighty Astrea*," and he comes from far-away regions of the Cosmic deep to help rid our cities of the entities that torment us.

Indeed, he is a veritable Pied Piper of Hamelin, who with magic flute lures away the evil psychic hordes infesting our townships, with or without sanction of the Lord Mayors, and with the Ballard "Children of Light" trailing joyfully in his wake.

According to Messenger Ballard, he came forth November 1st, 1937, on the stage of the auditorium in Philadelphia, where he announced his heroic mission.

"You will be interested to know," said he, "that they [the Ballard staff] have been calling for all black magicians and their emissaries to be sought out, seized and taken from the earth.

"Tonight, I have come forth to fulfill this call . . . That is why the Messenger saw entities going in every direction." (p. 141, A.M.L.)

Poor man! Rather disconcerting to see scampering armies of mischievous "entities," some perhaps more than mischievous, "*going in every direction!*" And this, despite the fact that Guy Ballard has so frequently insisted to his students that he is *not* a spiritualist, and sees *only* "Ascended Masters"!

Could the Mighty Astrea have slipped up in making this statement, or did the Messenger actually see Mighty Astrea routing "entities" out of Philadelphia?

However that may be, it was reported that "*over four hundred thousand discarnate entities*" were removed from the city of Philadelphia! And quite rightly, at so great a victory, the audience arose to its feet and applauded lustily! (p. 9, Jan., 1939, v.)

But this was only the start of the generalissimo's work. At the head of his grand army of many divisions, he has not let up one iota in his intention to clean the "entities" out of our cities. And from that time on, wherever the

Ballards went, Mighty Astrea and his entity-cleaning squad was sure to go.

Not to be left out of it, Saint Germain reported at the Washington class:

"Since yesterday *three hundred thirty-two thousand discarnates* were removed from the environs of New York City. (applause—audience standing)" (p. 8, Dec., 1938, v.)

A month later he adds up the net total for a single day, and reports to the applauding I AM-ers:

"In exactly twenty-three hours, *one million discarnates* have been taken from America. (applause)" And then he wisely adds: "It is necessary for you to take Our Word for these things for a short time." (pp. 26-27, Jan., 1939, v.)

We might here ask the question: "Why, with all this 'entity' clean-up, conditions in our cities and in the world continue as they do?" But, as usual, no explanation worthy of intelligence is ever given.

Nevertheless, Mighty Astrea's clean-up squad continues to mop-up the entity situation in our cities. He follows the Messengers around on their lecture tours and does what he can to have an entity-free city—even though the Lord Mayors of those cities pay him no tribute or acknowledge in any way his heroic services as a modern Pied Piper of Hamelin.

CHAPTER 8

METAPHYSICAL PLUMS

Clever leaders in political organizations know they must be lavish in scattering political plums among their adherents. They must also be prodigal in their promises, and wax eloquent in their statements concerning the marvelous benefits resulting should these favored ones become full-fledged members of the party.

It is similar with astute leaders of some metaphysical orders—and, certainly, the Ballard cult is no exception. Its metaphysical plum tree has been a marvelously productive one, so far as *promises* go, bearing luscious fruit and promising budlets within season and without. From a never-failing material supply in this life to tremendous power and influence in the life to come, the Ballard promises run the whole gamut of human desires.

Poor, struggling human mortals lost in the wilderness of a great economic depression! Who among them wouldn't want their "financial freedom" as promised by the Ballards?

Hearing such statements as, *"The precipitation of gold or jewels from the invisible to the visible is as simple as breathing"* (p. 97, D.)—they flock to the meetings as moths to the flame.

Reading such statements as, *"To you who have had a struggle financially . . . if you will only make your earnest application, I assure you that all obstruction will be removed from your pathway"* (p. 7, Dec., 1938, v.)—they buy the Ballard books, thinking that some magic formula will give them the money they need.

Pathetic, weak, sickly individuals looking so earnestly for health! How attracted they are to a cult which promises: "*You can renew any nerve, any organ, and build any member of the body into its perfection almost immediately.*" (p. 42, D.)

Or to the hopelessly old and decrepit, what a balm to hear: "*I say to you, beloved ones, who are in the neighborhood of sixty years old . . . I tell you—any one of you—in six weeks CAN be as strong, firm and active as you were in your fullest youth; but you must be determined.*" (p. 16, Sept., 1937, v.)

Oh, what a hope to the soul-sick individual who is tired of life and yet afraid to die, to hear a great Master say: "*There are quite a number in this room, who with complete harmony maintained, would make their Ascension in this embodiment.*" (p. 4, March, 1938, v.) These people were promised that if they made this so-called "Ascension," they would never die, or undergo physical death; that they would become "Ascended Masters"—or "Lady Masters"—immediately.

And to the frustrated and buffeted individual held down in the heavy morass of life, what an infinite blessing to hear: "*When this class at the Pan-Pacific Auditorium* [at Los Angeles] *is completed, there will be hundreds of you precious ones who will not again know limitation.*" (pp. 141-2, A. M. D.)

How credulous these students are to believe these, and many other, promises made so glibly, such as: "*There is not a single thing your heart can desire to do with this Instruction it cannot do . . . to cause the storm to cease and become obedient . . . to cause the rain to fall . . . to hold in abeyance the frost . . . etc., etc.,*" (pp. 28-33-34, March, 1937, v.)

In this way, by *promises*, and not by *works*, have the Ballards and their deceiving band of "Masters" attracted credulous people into their network of unreality.

What a cruel deception! These poor people give their money, their time, and their energies. They neglect their families and their opportunities, their health and perhaps even their spiritual salvation, by following a movement which will inevitably lead to sad disillusionment. And along the Ballard pathway there are hundreds of broken lives, wrecked homes, and an alarming number of insanity cases.

For over five years now the mills of these "Ascended Masters" have been grinding and turning out unbelievable promises. And the more they turned, the more the appetites of their people were whetted for the promised miracles.

Still, even among the unduly credulous, there is a limit to what people will take, as even the great Barnum discovered. So as time went on in the early days of the movement there was a noticeable restlessness among some of the students at the non-appearance of the scheduled miracles. Cleverly, to satisfy these people, the Ballards decided to make a few specific instances of attainment under the high promotion system of the great Ascended Master Saint Germain.

Therefore, preceding the Christmas holidays of 1936 there was circulated among the faithful veiled allusions as to the marvels that would take place at the coming "Shrine Class" in Los Angeles.

Word went forth that this was to be a "closed" class, open only to the elect. Transcendental things would occur. There were rumors of "group Ascensions," precipitated dinners, and some of the more popular "Ascended Masters" were scheduled to make tangible appearances. It was to be the outstanding metaphysical event of all time.

This had the effect, many months ahead, of giving the desired impetus and solidarity to the movement, which was then like a loose-jointed adolescent going through the teen age.

All roads led to the Los Angeles mecca, and around the middle of December, 1936, the pilgrimage was on. So great was the expectancy of the students for the promised miracles that many coming from eastern states brought along their *Ascension Robes!* A little precautionary measure which, by the way, was observed also rather widely in the City of the Angels among the faithful who did not want to be caught like the "foolish virgins" of a bygone age.

Of course all this was a good advertising build-up for the Accredited Messengers of Saint Germain, but it was a bit tricky. Realizing their inability to deliver the promises they had made, the leaders apparently became a little panic-stricken as to the reaction this might have if the scheduled miracles should be a little timid about showing up.

Therefore, there was a sudden change in plans. Edna Ballard, who usually can rise to the occasion, let it be known at a special meeting called just previous to the big "Shrine" opening, that it was not to be a "closed" meeting after all.

"All may come," she generously stated. "Fill the auditorium—but don't expect anything!"

And, of course, nothing did happen—other than more promises. Altogether it was a most tame affair. Not a single Ascended Master or precipitated dinner put in an appearance.

It was rumored around, however, that an "Ascended Master" was seen in the audience, and that he had talked privately to several of the Ballard staff members!

This is quite understandable in dear old Los Angeles where at any large heterodox meeting there is likely to be found one or more bewhiskered, longhaired, hermit-looking individuals who appear the living prototype of John the Baptist or Elijah the Prophet.

Also, among some of the students, there was a report

of another transcendent happening. Looking around for anything that might even give a semblance to a miracle, Guy Ballard suddenly stopped at a certain point in his talk, and listened. Audible to some, sounds of music floated in through the auditorium.

"If you will listen very carefully," said the heaven-gazing Messenger in an enraptured way, "you will hear something very interesting."

It was then reported among certain of the faithful in the audience that the fabled "Music of the Spheres" had been heard.

Some of the least susceptible ones, however, said it was merely syncopated jazz from a nearby skating rink. Others, even more skeptical, said it was somebody's radio played at a propitous time.

It is a strange and startling thing, however, and one which certainly shows the extent to which credulity exists in the world today, that despite all these failures throughout so many years the students are still waiting, waiting for the promised miracles. The whole process readily reminds one of the Raven—in Poe's poem of that name—"sitting, sitting above the chamber door," and forever quothing "Nevermore."

These Ballard miracles just didn't happen, never have, and it will take more than the Ballard family and all their king's horses to produce them.

However, the "Accredited Messengers" have learned to bring the promised miracles closer home to the poor students by vaguely referring to a certain number in each city who have made the grade in some way. In one city, for instance, Guy Ballard said:

"In this room tonight there are 104 for whom the Divine Director will consume the last vestige of human accumulation tonight." (March 11, 1938, Ballard Group Letter to Class Leaders.)

In another city, Cleveland, Ballard said:

"In this small audience, the human creation of 346 has been dissolved and consumed." (March 11, 1938, G. L.)

And so on with other audiences in various cities.

Nobody, of course, ever knows who these fortunate individuals are who have had their "*human creation*"—whatever that is—removed. It seems to have been kept a dark secret, not at all like some appendiceal operations. Each hopes that this human accumulation has been dissolved or extirpated in some way, but doubts must assail him when he discovers, despite the operation, that some remnants of the thing have been inadvertently left.

At the Kansas City class the statement was made:

" . . . For 373 of the students all human accumulation had been completely dissolved . . . for 283 *time* and *space* had been set aside!" (Feb. 18, 1938, G. L.)

Kansas City, it appears, wins the "human creation" honors; and, in addition, cleans up the entire running field in the Ballard "Time and Space" classic. How wonderful it must have been for these two hundred and eighty-three "Mighty I AM-ers" from Missouri to soar away—timeless and spaceless—into NOTHINGNESS, and be free from current bill collectors and future evils they know not of!

For reasons which we shall later discover, the Ballards for *four long years* did not hold public classes in their own home town after leaving there in the fall of 1934 to "Save America."

Although Chicago is undoubtedly a part of America, and needs saving perhaps as much as Los Angeles and Miami, there were good reasons why the wise and cautious "Saint Germain" did not for four years include that city in his Messengers' itinerary. There he was, titular head of a flourishing book concern—the "Saint Germain Press," with a perfectly good Chicago post office box number, and he was careless enough to forget to have his own Accredited Messengers lecture there to boost book sales.

The nearest city he would permit them to come, for a

public ten-day class, was Detroit. As a result, the Chicago faithful had to go to the automobile city to hear Saint Germain's Accredited Messengers—a modern instance, as it were, of the mountain going to Mahomet!

So in the spring of 1938 scores of the Chicago students traveled down railway ties or across macadamized roads bound for Detroit, to hear and learn from these modern prophets, whose symbol was the dazzling, golden "Light" of the sun, instead of the pale, silvery crescent of Mahomet.

They descended upon that mechanized city in such numbers that Prophet Ballard simply had to take notice of his people. It must have been very complimentary to him, and, of course, one good compliment deserves another.

So when they appeared in a festive body at the Scottish Rite Cathedral in Detroit to attend the Ballard class— somewhat as native Iowans congregate in Lincoln Park at Los Angeles for their annual get-together meeting—he looked them over and seeing their eagerness for one of the long promised miracles, was moved to say:

"Out of the number of Chicago people who have come to this class, one hundred of that number have had their own human creation dissolved and consumed in its completeness!" (page 11, June, 1938, v.)

What joy there must have been among these pilgrims from neglected Chicago who had sacrificed time and money for the journey. *One hundred* of them had had their "human creation" dissolved into thin air, or extirpated in some way by these miracle surgeons, the "Ascender Masters"—and not a single patient had succumbed, or had even been discommoded by the operation!

Then this modern prophet and dispenser of miracles looked away from the Chicago contingent, and gazed upon the Detroit gathering of the faithful. They, too, deserved something, some reward for their services; but some of them had been listening to things that all hundred-per-cent "I AM" students had been warned not to listen to. So, counting very rapidly, he said:

"Of those in Detroit, *twenty-seven* have had their entire human creation dissolved and consumed."

Only twenty-seven, as compared to Chicago's neat hundred. It just didn't seem fair, for Detroit too had turned out in large numbers. But, it appears, it was Detroit's own fault, for, said Prophet Ballard:

"Detroit has had a great opportunity; but because the students listened to very vicious gossip they have deprived themselves of this great, great opportunity."

However, offering a little encouragement to the losing team, he added:

"But still the Light shall claim Its own in Detroit! The Light shall claim Its own in Detroit! I so decree it!" (page 11, June, 1938, v.)

Poor Detroit! The Ballards wanted, for good reasons of their own as we shall discover, to shake the plum tree for their Chicago visitors at this class, but found it was a good opportunity also to penalize the Detroit students a little for disobedience in this little game of human creation.

Thus while they graciously shake the metaphysical plums off one limb, they none too graciously use another limb to whip the erring into line.

CHAPTER 9

THE BALLARD "ASCENSION" MIRACLES

Of all Ballard miracles, the one relating to the "Ascension" is perhaps the most alluring. It is the biggest plum of them all, and hangs higher on their miracle-bearing tree than all the others.

It is the Ballard answer to the ever-present problem of death, for when one makes the ascension, *he does not die!*

His physical body becomes charged with Light, and it "ascends" to become forever free from the limitations of birth and death. He then becomes, according to the Ballard idea, an *"Ascended Master,"* able to roam the corporeal and incorporeal worlds at will.

Of course, the idea is not new. It has been and is a part of many religious philosophies, varying only in details.

All their students have to do, it appears, is to be obedient to the "Ascended Masters" and their three and only "Accredited Messengers," sweep an imaginary *"Violet Consuming Flame"* through their bodies morning, noon, and night for the necessary purification, and then call most vehemently for their ascension. The Ballards have virtually guaranteed their faithful and obedient students their ascension in this life!

One suspects, therefore, this ascension business is but another lure to gain converts, and we believe evidence for this belief will be amply justified in this chapter.

In *Unveiled Mysteries*, the hero—Godfrey Ray King—recounts how he, personally, assisted an "old man with white hair and beard" to make his ascension from the side of Mt. Shasta, California.

He had just given the tired, discouraged old man a drink from a *"Crystal Cup"* which formed miraculously in Godfre's hand, when lo! without warning the man began to rise from the ground all clothed in a "raiment of Glistening White," and then *"disappeared on a Radiant Pathway of Light!"* (p. 242, U. M.)

The experience naturally made a profound impression upon our hero, who of course was none other than Guy Ballard of Chicago. And he has been thinking and acting this "Ascension" drama ever since.

In Godfre's next book, *The Magic Presence*, he describes a couple of other ascensions, but instead of using the potent drink in the same "Crystal Cup," he brought in the idea of a mechanical device known as the *"Atomic Accelerator"*—a marvelous golden chair which in some way, by merely sitting in it, helps the weary neophyte to make the final journey into the heavens.

Time was when the initiatory process was an arduous one, but in the Ballard system one just sits and sits in a golden chair. It is as easy as that!

Such a device is alleged to be in Saint Germain's secret retreat in the Wyoming Rockies, the "Cave of Symbols." And here one day, Ballard and his party arrive to observe the "Ascension" of a "white-haired elderly gentleman" by name of David, who for some reason or other was privileged to sit in the golden Atomic Accelerator.

Well, as might be expected, it wasn't long before David's *"hair had returned to its original color, dark brown, the lines faded from his face, his flesh became the pink of perfect health, and his beard disappeared."* (p. 84, M. P.)

But more marvelous of all, the whole of David himself soon disappeared in a "dazzling radiance" of Light. Thus is described ascension No. 2.

Ascension No. 3 was that of his friend and fellow traveler, Rayborn, the wealthy ranch owner, who was soon to say goodbye to all his cattle and gold mines and sit in the golden Atomic Accelerator.

Ballard and his party arrive according to schedule, as likewise do the "Ascended Masters" and some lovely "Lady Masters," among whom is numbered Rayborn's "Twin Ray."

All is in readiness. The spectators take their positions, and the western cattle king sits in the golden accelerator.

In a few moments, it is all over. Rayborn ascends clear through the ceiling of the cave and disappears with his Twin Ray, while "like a flash of lightning, a circle of the most intense, dazzling, white Light" encompasses the entire place. (p. 288, M. P.) Thus did the cattle king make his "Ascension."

Now, when any one of the Ballard family can make an ascension like this, or the two before, then we will more readily believe in the Ballard "Ascension Miracles."

Already, Mr. Ballard has claimed he has had such an opportunity, but for reasons best known to himself did not chose to ascend. He did, however, he says, sit in the golden Atomic Accelerator and it had the effect of making him "want to jump right out of the body"!

The reason Mr. Ballard did not choose to make his ascension is allegedly as follows. We quote his remarks made at Los Angeles on the afternoon of August 25, 1935:

"Saint Germain insists that I mention something that I have never mentioned even to my blessed family. Before Mrs. Ballard starts to read about the ascension of Mr. Rayborn, of which I have spoken, I want to say this:

"At the time of Mr. Rayborn's ascension I was given the opportunity to make the ascension, but the Mighty 'I AM' Presence said: 'No! Go back into the world and serve.'

"That hour my earthly pilgrimage was finished. Since that time I am here in this atomic structure on extended time . . . *Nothing this human form can do can be recorded on my Life stream.*

"I know there will be those who will go forth and say possibly, 'That's just a little bit of drama.' Beloved ones, I would be *removed from this embodiment* if I said one word that was not true."

It is certainly one of the magic workings of this man's life that he has the ability of making people believe in him. Against logic and common sense, despite contradictions and misstatements, and in the face of absurdity after absurdity, his followers believe the statements that he makes.

At still another time, while assertedly in India, at Chananda's Secret Retreat in the Himalayas, he said he had the opportunity of making his ascension, but again, his "I AM" told him to go back into the world and serve.

Edna Ballard, also, has had her opportunity, but like her self-sacrificing husband, she refused her ascension, too. We quote "Saint Germain's" statement made at Philadelphia on May 9, 1937:

"The Beloved Messengers here, when they came back from Honolulu could have said Good-bye to you and have gone on, but they did not! Their Love was great enough to go on, and on, facing and conquering the viciousness which has been projected at them." (page 8, A. M. L.)

But could not these people have served and conquered better by *making* their "Ascensions"?

We are curious enough to wonder whether the Ballards will use the "Crystal Cup" and make their ascensions from the side of Mt. Shasta, or will they make use of the more scientific "Atomic Accelerator" and ascend through the ceiling at the Cave of Symbols in Wyoming. Only time can tell.

The Ballard Ascension miracles have lured thousands of old people to the fold. But after four years of promises without a single ascension, even the most Ballardized of the students began to wonder if any of them would ever make their ascensions, or, for that matter, ever sit in the golden chair for just a few moments.

Therefore, the resourceful Messengers evidently decided that instead of making more promises, they had better produce a few ascensions. So out of a clear sky one evening, on the Ides of March, at Cleveland, they announced to a thrilled audience:

"On next Sunday, there will be ten Ascensions!" (p. 3, April, 1938, v.)

But alas! Clevelandites were soon to learn that these ascensions were not to be made in their fair city. They were to be made at Saint Germain's private and quite inaccessible mountain retreats: "Five from the Cave of Symbols" and "Five from the Retreat in Arabia."

Imagine the consternation of those who could not leave their businesses to go to Wyoming or to far-away Arabia!"

They had been told the "Ascension" had to be made in an actual *physical* body. And it had to be a living body, not a dead one. But none of these students knew how to take their bodies to the Cave of Symbols in Wyoming, and certainly not to the retreat in the fastnesses of the Arabian mountains.

Incidentally, two of the other alleged secret retreats, the one at Mt. Shasta, California, and the "Royal Teton" in Wyoming, have been the occasion for a number of foolish pilgrimages of the students. There are authentic stories of students who have given up their families, their positions, their money, and have camped outside the rocky portals of Mt. Shasta in California and the Grand Teton in Wyoming, waiting for the respective mountain to open up and let them in. It had for Guy Ballard—why not for them!

A friend writes from the Grand Teton National Park that he had talked to the postmistresses at Moose, Wyoming, at the base of the Grand Teton; the postmistress at Jenny Lake; also to forest rangers and others; and found, "the same old story":

"I AM students, queer people . . . looking for the pot

of gold at the end of the rainbow.

"Yes, quite a few of them come up here . . . Leave disillusioned . . . one was killed on his way back home after waiting a year for the mountain to open up . . . Another was placed in the State Insane Asylum here . . . etc."

Getting back to the announcement at Cleveland; even though the students were never told *who* the lucky ten were who made their ascensions, it had the effect of arousing hope and renewed efforts among the faithful students, and made them even more obedient than before to the Ballards and their "Ascended Masters."

But in time, after a few more "Ascensions" of this order, the *private* ascension idea began to play out, and the Ballards for that and other reasons too were compelled to institute a *totally different kind of ascension* than previously described in their books.

One of these reasons is most obvious. The Ballards themselves were getting older, and the strain of their work was telling upon them. Therefore, they had to make their ascension promises fit any eventuality that might occur in their own lives.

Then, again, for years, their students had been dying, leaving the *mortal coil behind*—a clear proof the promised ascension had *not* taken place!

In some way this "proof" had to be concealed or rendered unimportant in some way. The following is a description of the way they attempted to do it.

Despite the fact that they had formerly most emphatically stated the ascension could *only* be made by "raising" the actual PHYSICAL body, and then only *before* death occurred, they now had the resourceful but none-too-consistent Saint Germain come through with a startling and unprecedented message. A message which completely changed the effect and intent of their original *inviolate* "Ascension Law."

"Beloved Children of the Light," said Saint Germain

on November 8, 1938, at Washington, D. C., "I want you to see and feel the Reward which Life has chosen to give to certain individuals . . . In all ages past, the Ascension could only be made by taking the purified physical body into the Higher Mental Body, as the Messenger has explained to you." (p. 5, Dec., 1938, v.)

Then Saint Germain told how a *"New Dispensation"* had been arranged for the faithful students!

It seems that two fair members of the "Ascended Master" hierarchy—the "Goddess of Light" and the "Goddess of Liberty"—went personally to a great Being, *"Sanat Kumara,"* sitting somewhere in the heavens, to intercede in the Ballard students' behalf.

It appears further that this great Being, Sanat Kumara, giving in to the entreaties of two beautiful goddesses, agreed to take special pity on the plight of Ballard students, who, instead of making their ascensions as they were promised, were dying and leaving their bodies behind.

The outcome of the heavenly conclave was—as Saint Germain so clearly explains—*there will now be "certain ones among the students" who will be "permitted to make the Ascension while the outer structure, the discord of human form, remains here."*

Now that this troublesome little matter of the "physical remains" has been solved in this heavenly fashion, it seems reasonable to suspect this new kind of ascension will occur by the wholesale.

And sure enough, in the second issue of their magazine following this stupendous announcement of the "New Dispensation" authorized by a *single* individual sitting in his high heaven, we see in purple print that the Ballard ascension mills are already beginning to grind!

As evidence of this, we quote the "Great Divine Director's remarks made at the Shrine Class in Los Angeles on January 8, 1939:

"Already in three different instances, those, who have

made the change, which others not understanding thought was so-called death, have made the Ascension. In each instance there has not been one particle of Life remaining in the cells or structure of the flesh that remained behind, which is mechanical evidence of the Truth that they had made the Ascension. There are quite a number who will make that change within a few months . . . it can easily and readily be done." (pp. 19-20, Feb., 1939, v.)

This kind of ascension, *"so easily and readily accomplished,"* is no doubt all right for any of the *un*-Accredited Messengers, class leaders, and obedient students, but for the three and only *"Accredited Messengers,"* surely the more difficult ascension under the old dispensation is required.

We therefore expect that the Ballards will stage at least one, if not, three good, old-fashioned ascensions such as described in their books, and ascend heavenward *physically* and *corporeally* either by way of the "Crystal Cup" or the "Atomic Accelerator"!

And when they do that, we and the other doubting Thomases of the land will believe in the Ballard "Ascension Miracles."

CHAPTER 10

COSMIC STREAMLINE ADVERTISING

During the time Guy and Edna Ballard have been presenting their Mighty I AM teachings to "America and the World," they have used advertising methods and a showmanship which could teach even the late P. T. Barnum a trick or two. Instead of having a raucous-voiced old showman come forth to harangue the crowd as to the particular merits of the performance and the wonders to be seen, the Ballards have no less a personage than some high and mighty *"Cosmic Master"* shout the praises of the show.

Let the de luxe advertising clubs of the land take note. The best they have done is to get some glamorous Hollywood star to praise the merits of somebody's brand of cigarettes or face cream. It remained for two heretofore unknown Chicago persons to get the *stars in the firmament* to advertise for them and sing paeans of praises concerning their products.

A great "Star-Being," known as *"Arcturus,"* has come forward from cosmic space and has okayed the Ballard show and all the actors in it.

A "Mighty Being" from the planet Venus, traveling some twenty-six million miles to attend a speaking engagement in Los Angeles, has sung Venusian praises about the "Accredited Messengers of Saint Germain," delivered in quite ordinary English, with a few slang expressions thrown in.

A "Great Being" beyond the "Central Sun" of the universe has even taken note of the delectable merits of

Saint Germain's precipitated dinners, ascension robes, and what not, and has come forward after a million years of silence to boost the sale of the Ballard books and merchandise.

"We have not used," say Mr. and Mrs. Ballard, "the *outer world's* methods of advertising to gain the attention of anyone or draw students to us." (p. 20, Aug., 1938, v.)

No, indeed! What they have done is to scour the world invisible for personal supporters to their hoax. They brought forth such singular names as "Mighty Victory," the "Great Tenor," the "God Meru," the "Lady Master Nada," the "Tall Master from Venus," the "Old Man of the Hills," and thirty others of equally good advertising value. They even signed the name of *"Jesus the Christ"* to some of their sales talks!

In introducing the Ballards to their audiences, their stage announcer and chief earth-plane advertising man has many times said:

"These wonderful people, beloved ones, are occupying the place that Jesus the Christ did two thousand years ago!"

And later, when some of the contradictions in their writings and statements were pointed out, they had this same "Jesus" say:

"These Beloved Messengers have not made one single mistake from the beginning." (p. 15, Feb., 1937, v.)

They had Jesus' most loved disciple, *"John the Beloved,"* allegedly come forth for the first time since his death to say of the Ballards:

"There never were two such interested, selfless human beings on the face of this earth as the Messengers are." (p. 13, Feb., 1938, v.)

Not being willing to let their greatness speak silently for itself, or perhaps being a trifle dubious about it themselves, the Ballards had an "Ascended Master" known as *"The Great Divine Director,"* whom they solemnly assert is the teacher of Jesus, say:

"This Work the Messengers are giving is the Greatest that will ever be given on earth!" (p. 17, Dec., 1937, v.)

Then to add an element of mystery as to who and what they really are, these "Mighty I AM" magicians brought forth out of their bag of cosmic tricks the *Tall Master from Venus.*" This tall Venusian gentleman with long golden hair, not being able, it seems, to use his own vocal cords, made use of Guy Ballard's, and got quite a bit of applause from the large audience at the Shrine Auditorium in Los Angeles on the evening of July 17, 1938, when he said:

"I call your attention to these beloved Messengers, the most precious Beings on the face of this earth today. Look how they struggled for years just like the rest of mankind; and look today! . . .

"They are free Beings today and *could leave you at any moment;* but their great Love will not let that be done at present. (applause) . . . *You do not yet know who is in your midst; you might be greatly amazed one day when we tell you.*" (p. 11, Sept., 1938, v.)

Just who it was in their midst was at first a cherished secret among informed I AM-ers, and they mentioned it with bated breath, but it wasn't long before Guy Ballard himself was publicly advertising to the whole country that he was none other than the reincarnated *George Washington,* the traditional "Father of Our Country"!

And so Ballard has since been known, quite appropriately it seems, as *"Daddy Ballard"*—and his Blessed Lotus, as *"Mamma Ballard"!*

The subject of past incarnations among the members of this blue-blooded Ballard family is most illuminating and even exciting. Quite naturally, it is to be expected that Edna Lotus Ray King Ballard's reincarnations would be equally as famous as those of her illustrious husband's. And we find that that is so.

Edna, however, is *not* the reincarnated Martha Washington, as might be expected. "Saint Germain" has chosen a more dramatic and heroic role for the present George Washington's ambitious wife. And so we learn that Edna is none other than the French heroine, *Joan of Arc, sainted Savior of France!*

And to properly advertise the fact, the *Archangel Michael* (!) came forward from far-away cosmic space to confirm the present Joan's identity by saying:

"I have not ministered to earth since My Ministry in France. I ministered then to the same individual who, this night, I begin to minister through in America, our beloved Joan of Arc." (p. 5, Jan., 1939, v.)

The third and last member of this illustrious Ballard family is of course, Donald Ray King Ballard. Here also we find a remarkable history of past achievement. Donald was born into the world on May 12, 1918, in the city of Chicago, as *Edona Eros Ballard*. That is exactly the name which appears on the official certificate of birth. In a former earth life he was King of the Incas, and in one more recent he was the distinguished nobleman, *Marquis de Lafayette of France!*

Now that we have the Ballard reincarnation tree duly established, and properly advertised, we believe the threefold combination will prove to be rather thought provoking—for we now have *Washington,* the Father of our Country, *Joan,* the Savior of France, and *Lafayette,* dashing young friend of the American Revolution, all right here in our midst!

These three, and the other more numerous but less illustrious members of the "Mighty I AM" family, numbering some hundreds of thousands strong, are here to "Save America" and bring in a "New Government" in the good old U. S. A.

We wonder what were the thoughts of the trio when, on a trip to Washington, they visited George and Martha's old homestead at Mt. Vernon? We wonder what they thought about when they drove down historic Pennsylvania Avenue in their expensive platinum-tinted car, passed the White House, and headed for the Capitol?

We do not know, of course, but we have it from "Saint Germain" himself (speaking at the Rialto Auditorium in Wasington on November 8, 1938) that "These two (meaning Joan and George) . . . are as humble as humbleness can be . . . Without them mankind would have been in the most seething vortex of war right in your midst today. Your Capital would not be here today!" (p. 6, Dec., 1938, v.)

All of which somehow reminds us of the childhood story of George Washington and the cherry tree, and the little boy who could not tell a lie.

On authority of no less a personage than the *"Archangel Michael,"* the U. S. A. will fare a good deal better with her reincarnated Lotus Ray King Ballard than did France with her martyred Jeanne d'Arc, for in keeping with the story books, the heroine lives instead of meeting an untimely end.

"That blessed one," says the Archangel (meaning Mrs. Ballard), "who was once burned at the stake, will not be this time. (applause)" (p. 20, Jan., 1939, v.) Which, of course, in anyone's life is a reassuring thing to know.

But the *"Goddess of Liberty"* is even more eulogistic of this remarkable "I AM" family than is the more conservatively-speaking Archangel Michael. At their great Shrine Class in Los Angeles, on Sunday afternoon, January 2, 1938, this magnificent feminine deity reportedly "came forth" to say to an applauding audience:

"We can tell you, every one of you, in the embodiments where you were in association with the Messengers, and how you came again and again, giving the same loyalty . . . We won't go back far, but in the time of Richard the Lion-hearted in England, again Joan of Arc in France, again Washington, and again today, you stand, and have stood through the Ages with that Loyalty to the Light and to those Precious Ones [the Ballards] who represented the Light . . . Let Me call you 'Our Sweethearts of America,' for *without you* MANKIND WOULD PERISH FROM THE EARTH!

"And *but for these Messengers* MANKIND WOULD HAVE PERISHED FROM THE EARTH!" (Jan. 7, 1938, G. L.)

Today, these same Ballard "Sweethearts" actually believe that George and Joan, or "Blessed Mamma and Daddy Ballard," are the saviors of mankind, and will bring a new government to the United States of America.

Can the reader contemplate what is happening to the intelligence of an astounding number of American citizens who accept as gospel truth the crudely devised personal advertisements of a Chicago couple?

CHAPTER 11

VOYAGES OF A MODERN SINDBAD

In A.D. 1934 the metaphysical world was startled by the appearance of an occult thriller, entitled *Unveiled Mysteries,* copyrighted by the Saint Germain Press, P. O. Box 1133, Chicago, Ill.

In it is narrated a series of fantastic occult adventures of one Godfre Ray King, which adventures, the foreword says, are as "*Real and True as mankind's existence on this earth today.*"

The first page of this "true account" of the adventures of Godfre Ray King informs us that he "knew through travels in the Far East, that most rumors, myths, and legends have, somewhere as their origin, a deep underlying Truth."

And then with *himself* as the living hero of it all, he proceeds to bring the adventures of Sindbad the Sailor, the incredible tales of Baron Munchausen, the travels of Gulliver, and other "rumors, myths, and legends" together as the one "deep underlying Truth."

All story tellers have a way with them. It is said that the estimable old gentleman, the Baron Munchausen, would never crack a smile as he related the most incredible of his tales, and he did it so well that some of his hearers were even persuaded to believe he meant his fantastic stories to be taken seriously!

Perhaps he did. One's wildest imaginings assume a semblance of reality if they are re-created often enough. At any rate the genial old Baron, or his narrator, in an effort to vindicate his stories and his own veracity, attached to his manuscript a notice to the public affirming the absolute truth of his stories. It was signed by *Gulliver*, *Sindbad*, and *Aladdin*, and was to the effect that they personally attested that the adventures of their friend, the Baron Munchausen, were "positive and simple facts"—the affidavit being duly sworn at the City of London, England, before "John the Porter" in the absence of the Lord Mayor.

Similarly, the modern author of fabulous literature, Godfre Ray King, like the truth-loving old Baron, attests to his own veracity by saying in his foreword that his adventures are "Real and True." But he goes the Baron one better by bringing forth, instead of the reputable Gulliver, Sindbad, and Aladdin, no less a personage than the credible "*Saint Germain*," who swears to the truth in these books in his own vehement way; and, as though his word were not sufficient, proceeds to bring forth the whole "Cosmic Host" to back him up.

Assured by this testimony we can now with more confidence follow the narrator through his series of surprising adventures beginning on the slanting slopes of Mt. Shasta, California, and ending in a marvelous cave in the Grand Teton Mountain in Wyoming, where a tall golden-haired gentleman from our sister planet Venus gives him some sage advice.

The very first day that Godfre met the mysterious Count St. Germain on a California mountain side, time passed all too quickly, as you can imagine it would if a great Master showed you your past embodiments, including one where you were a priest and your present wife a "*vestal virgin guarding the Sacred Fire.*" (p. 25, U. M.)

So as Godfre was ten miles away from his lodge at the foot of the mountain and it would be nearly midnight before he could return on foot, the great "Master" obligingly offered him another means of locomotion.

"Place your arm about my shoulder," said he, "and close your eyes."

"I felt my body lifted from the ground," relates God-fre in telling of this amazing transportation of his actual physical body through space, and added: "Presently, my feet touched the floor and opening my eyes—I stood in the lodge."

Commenting on Godfre's question as to how it was possible to come back in this manner without attracting the attention of others, the great "Master" explains:

"We many times draw about our bodies the cloak of invisibility when moving among those in physical form." And the next second, Godfre writes, "he was gone." (pp. 27-28, U. M.)

We can imagine the humorous old Baron sitting around the tavern table with congenial spirits telling such a tale as this, and we can hear the laughter of those around him while the old fellow snorts at their disbelief. But, alas, in this modern age, strange as it may seem, disbelief in such fabulous narratives has turned to *belief* in the case of many hundreds of thousands of adult Americans!

Godfre's book might well have been entitled: "A Continuation of the Surprising Adventures of Baron Munchausen" or "The Occult Adventures of Sindbad the Sailor."

However, some of the tales are hardly suitable as bedtime stories. One of them, at least, is the thriller type, and red blood is spilled.

One day while walking along a mountain trail at Mt. Shasta, our hero is attacked successively by a "vicious-eyed panther" and a "considerably heavier mountain lion." The former he has calmed by looking commandingly into its eyes, and before the latter could rend him in its leap, the panther whom he had tamed by the magnetism of his eyes protects him by leaping upon the mountain lion. Then both animals die in a terrific struggle, but Godfre, the hero, is saved.

Baron Munchausen in his own surprising adventures tells a somewhat similar story. He is attacked successively, but not successfully, by a ferocious lion and a forty-foot crocodile. The lion springs at him, but at the right moment the Baron *ducks,* causing the lion to leap into the gaping jaws of the crocodile who is attacking the Baron from the rear. Both animals die in the resulting terrific struggle, and Munchausen escapes with his skin—he taking the lion's skin instead!

Incredible as this crocodile story of the Baron's may seem to the unenlightened, we have in America stories just as thrilling, which, although they may be rejected and scoffed at by the uninformed, are nevertheless believed by enlightened I AM-ers who read and re-read Godfre Ray King's amazing books.

Perhaps the most thrilling of the tales in Godfre's first book is the one in which he tells how he got back into his embalmed body of seventy thousand years ago!

This body had been miraculously preserved all those seven hundred centuries, but instead of it having the cadaveric appearance of a mummified Rameses II, it had retained all its original state of youth and beauty, looking most lifelike with its long "wavy golden hair" and dressed in a "golden fabric" of marvelous beauty.

In this body, which had all the youthful appearance of a golden-haired Apollo, the then fifty-two year old Godfre functioned for an hour or so, until the clock struck twelve at the Palace of the Masters, at which time, like Cinderella of the fairy tales, he slipped back into his old garments of flesh, to become once again the most famous of twentieth-century occult adventurers and story tellers.

This midnight cadaveric experience of Godfre Ray King was not quite so ghostly as one would think. It was really a gala event not only for Godfre but for the entire Ray King family. Edna Lotus Ray King and Edona Eros Ray King (then a boy of twelve) arrive also for the event. And not to be outdone by Godfre, they have beautifully embalmed bodies of their own, which they succeed in raising from their "crystal caskets" after 70,000 years of sleep. Then the three Kings walk around admiring and complimenting one another. (p. 249, U. M.)

In such matters as these, there is certainly safety and security in numbers, as those of us well know, who, in the old days, walked through the churchyard cemetery on a dark night with the ancestral dead all about us. Still, as a conscientious reviewer, we would not advise some of Godfre's tales as strictly bedtime stories for children.

The Magic Presence is a continuation of Godfre's marvelous experiences. It starts with his visit to the Diamond K Ranch in Wyoming, and from then on he makes almost as many voyages as did Sindbad the Sailor, eventually landing in far-away India, where he brings to life the old Arabian Nights Entertainment tale of *"The Magic Carpet."*

Actually—literally and corporeally—he gets on one with his two physical feet, which he describes as a "gorgeous Persian silk rug of a most wonderful golden yellow."

And away he flies, off into the Himalayan stratosphere on a non-stop, no-gasoline flight, just as easily as you please, and comes down without mishap from "eleven thousand feet above the palace!" (p. 381, M. P.)

Having had considerable experience in sailing off the side of Mt. Shasta on Saint Germain's power and landing in his lodge at the foot of the mountain, as well as sailing off Himalayan mountain tops on "Magic Carpets" to the ambient air above, he was offered the opportunity while in India of making one last voyage.

In other words, the opportunity of making his "Ascension"—soaring off physically and permanently into the "Seventh Octave of Light," thereby becoming an "Ascended Master."

But, as we have seen, he decided against it, saying that his "I AM" wanted him to come back to the world and serve.

And so Godfre came back to America again, but rides no longer upon magic carpets. Alas, in this mundane occidental land the nearest thing to a magic carpet is a transcontinental airline plane, but most of the time it is the gas and steam car for this most famous of world travelers.

It is seldom that a weaver of fantastic yarns gets away with so much true-story acclaim as has Godfre Ray King. Yet, there have been some historic examples of this kind of thing, and each age seems to have them. The people of one generation revolt at learning the lessons of the preceding generation, and must, it seems, experience the whole thing over again.

As an example of this, we shall quote one from the past, which, in a sense, may remind us of the amazing adventures of Godfre Ray King.

Just at the tail-end of the 19th century, the famous traveler and adventurer, *Louis de Rougemont,* appeared in London fresh from the cannibalistic wilds of Australia. He astounded the scientific circles of that day by his erudite knowledge of aboriginal life, for he had actually lived for thirty years among the savages of the Australian bush, and had in fact become their cannibal chief. However, making his escape, he presented himself before certain scientific societies and made the acquaintance of the editor of a British journal, all of whom listened with attentive ear to his adventures.

The *Wide World Magazine* of August, 1898, wrote up the story, which was described as "the most amazing story a man ever lived to tell." As a result, they received "shoals of letters" daily asking whether the adventurer would "afford the British public an opportunity of seeing him in the flesh."

Meanwhile, letters had been pouring in to the British paper, the *Daily Chronicle,* voicing a rising skepticism. But M. de Rougemont answered his critics with the certain conviction gained through his thirty years experiences among the cannibals, and at his public lectures denounced his detractors in no uncertain terms.

The sequel to this amazing story of the adventures of Louis de Rougemont in the wilds of Australia will now, with regret, have to be given. We quote directly, in part, from its sad ending, as published by Frederick A. Stokes Company in their book, "SOBER TRUTH—A Collection of Nineteenth-century Episodes, Fantastic, Grotesque and Mysterious," compiled and edited by Margaret Barton and Osbert Sitwell:

"Then the *Daily Chronicle*, after having made exhaustive enquiries, published what it claimed (and proved) to be the true story of de Rougemont's life. Alas, he had never been a cannibal chief, for the loftiest position he had ever occupied was that of butler to a Lady Robinson in Australia . . . In the spring of 1898 he landed in this country [England], and, after spending some weeks in the reading room of the British Museum, studying, no doubt, books of travel and adventure, presented himself to the Editor of the *Wide World Magazine* as 'Louis de Rougemont,' the cannibal chief. He was received with open arms, and for a brief space enjoyed fame and prosperity as a nineteenth-century Robinson Crusoe. After his exposure, he fled to Suchy, and oblivion descended on him from the day he was seen there, sitting in a cafe, apparently wrapped in gloomy contemplation."

It is to be expected from what is known of human nature that as the twentieth century fades into oblivion and a new century dawns, we shall still have adventurers and narrators such as Godfre Ray King, Louis de Rougemont, Munchausen, et al, telling strange and amazing stories of their adventures into the Land of Make-Believe.

Is it too much to hope, however, that the public of that day will be better able to discern fact from fiction than has apparently the large number of people who have lived in the preceding and present centuries?

CHAPTER 12

THE COMTE DE ST. GERMAIN—HISTORICAL AND OTHERWISE

We come now to a consideration of odd fact and fancy, which will show to what extent the human mind loves the mysteriousness that oftentimes enshrouds itself over the lives of notable characters.

Human traits are forgotten in all this mysteriousness, and such individuals are made the synthesis of all that is strange, odd, fantastic, incredible, and miraculous. Far removed from the standpoint of time and perhaps of place, mankind looks back upon them and makes of them, gods, heroes, and saints.

It is with such a thought as this that we can, perhaps, best introduce that enigmatical character of the 18th century known as the Comte de St. Germain.

Encyclopædic writers are decidedly less approving of the Count than are novelists and occultists. We have therefore two versions or interpretations of this remarkable man. One of the encyclopaedists refers to him as "the most celebrated mystic adventurer of modern times." Another calls him a "charlatan," a "deceiver," an "extraordinary impostor."

But occultists and romancers almost without exception call him an "adept," a "transcendental magician," a "Messenger of the Great White Lodge," and so on—depending upon the shade and character of belief residing in the writer.

One of the occult writers on the subject points out that "we must cast aside the theories that M. de St. Germain was a homeless and penniless adventurer, seeking to make money out of any kindly disposed person." (*The Comte de St. Germain,* p. 15, by I. Cooper-Oakley.)

"No obscure adventurer is this," says this writer, "but a man of princely blood and almost royal descent."

The Count St. Germain is reputed by some authorities to have been one of the sons of Prince Franz-Leopold Ragoczy of Transylvania, who had received land grants from Louis XV. If this be so, then the Count had wealth and title in his own right. Opinions, however, differ as to his parentage. And as to his name, there were many that he went by, the "Comte de St. Germain" being but one of a dozen or more.

This fact has been used, says Mrs. Cooper-Oakley, to militate against his honesty and integrity. She points out that this was the practice among persons of rank and title in that day to escape vulgar curiosity. It was no doubt done also for political reasons, his own inherited name from the Ragoczy line being politically dangerous.

The present-day exhibitors of the Count, the two Ballards, have for their own purposes brought him out of rusty encyclopædias and occult tomes, and have popularized his name among millions. They ignore, however, his other cognomens, titles, and prefixes and give him a name of their own—"The Ascended Master Saint Germain." They emphasize the "Saint" part of the name by spelling it always out in full, instead of its accustomed abbreviated form.

This has served to make some think he was canonized by the Roman Church, when of course he wasn't at all, the name "St. Germain" being but a family name. We have used generally the Ballard way of spelling out the name, especially when we refer to Ballards' man Friday instead of to the real and historic Comte de St. Germain.

Whatever we may think of this man as an "adventurer," a "charlatan," a "deceiver," we shall nevertheless have to concede that here was a man of some real genius. Even the encyclopædias who refer to him as a charlatan, at the same time speak of him as learned in many of the arts and sciences of that day. They say he knew many languages; that he spoke, fluently, German, English, Italian, French, Portuguese, and Spanish; that his diction and grammar were *flawless*. (Let the *Ballard* Saint Germain take notice!)

He was an accomplished musician, and could play the piano divinely, as well as being more than a dabbler in oils. He was an unusual chemist for those times, and sought to transmute the baser metals into gold, which was the end of the chemist's art of that period. It was even claimed that he had some success in that direction, as well as producing the greatest alchemical feat of all, the "Philosopher's Stone."

He seems always to have been well supplied with money, and displayed to his friends and intimates many diamonds and precious stones. Removing flaws from diamonds appears to have been his special hobby, along with his predilection for wearing diamonds in his shoe buckles. Perhaps, though, that was the thing to do in those days, just as only a few years ago it was the fashion for the well-dressed man to wear a pin in his necktie.

The Count was a story-teller of note, but that he at times went over to the imaginative and fanciful is doubtlessly true. He claimed to have been on intimate terms with the Queen of Sheba, Solomon, Paracelsus, and a few other notables, even going back as far as the traditional Melchizedek, King of Salem and Priest of the Most High God who met Abraham in the valley of Shaveh.

His memory seems a little long for this present age, but who can say how far we shall be able to go back into the past some day by strictly scientific means?

The belief in these things, and the possibility of them, is taken advantage of by the charlatan and the story-teller. We hope the entertaining Count was able to go back that far, but it is well to be just a little skeptical

about such things when we still have a few modern Munch-
ausens and Sindbads in the world.

Louis XV of France had an especial fondness for the
Comte St. Germain. He fitted up an apartment for him
at his royal Chateau of Chambord, and assigned him a
wing in his palace for a chemical laboratory. The Count
was a friend and adviser to many notables of that day,
including Prince Karl of Hesse, the ill-fated Marie Antoi-
nette, and it seems, also to Catherine the Great of Russia.

It appears that he had many missions into foreign lands,
and some believe he was an international spy. If he was
an adventurer and nothing more, it is seldom that such a
character continues to have the patronage of kings and
princes for so long a time as did the Count. His name was
a byword, well spoken, on the continent and in England.

But he had his enemies, too. Carlisle wasn't fond of his
popularity; Casanova said he was a simple impostor; and
Voltaire spoke rather contemptuously of him, remarking:
"He is a man who never dies, and who knows everything."

By his political enemies he was considered a dangerous
character, and orders one time were issued for him to be
bound hand and foot and taken to the Bastille. He, however, escaped to England. So it was—and is today—not
altogether an easy task to live the life of a "Mystery Man."

The Comte de St. Germain is said to have dressed with
becoming taste—snuff-box, watch, jewels, buckles, and all.
The finest diamonds flashed from his person. The ladies
of that day were particularly fond of him, as can be
imagined, but no scandal attached to his name. He gave
them cosmetics and an elixir to keep age away, and that
seemed to suffice.

His manners were elegant, his hair black, and his eyes
soft and penetrating. He always dressed in black satin,
which fact goes a little contrary to the Ballard picture of
"Saint Germain" dressed in white, or sometimes wearing
a purple cape. The Ballard "Saint Germain" hates black,

but the 18th-century one wore it constantly.

An original portrait of the Count, by Thomas, is in the Louvre, dated 1783, and inscribed: "Marquis Saint Germain der Wundermann." This shows him to be a clean-shaven man with a white wig, dressed in black velvet with white vest and ruffles.

It looks no more like the portrait of the Ballard Saint Germain, as painted by Charles Sindelar, than a smooth-shaven man would look beside the bearded George Bernard Shaw.

And neither of these two pictures look anything like the *first* portrait of Saint Germain which appeared originally in the Ballard books. So we have the spectacle of three totally different-appearing St. Germains. The reader can take his choice from the lot. The writer chooses the Louvre exhibit as being slightly more authentic, and the wig a trifle more judicial, than the two others.

The Count traveled much—but did not, it seems, use the astral streamlined method such as he is supposed to use today. The boat and coach were good enough.

In various countries he assumed different names, usually names of rank and nobility, but always appeared to be a man of about fifty years. Quite appropriately, it seems, this "Mystery Man" claimed descent from the Ragoczy line in Transylvania, for Transylvania is said by some occultists to be one of the most mysterious countries in the world—but certainly, today, has its troubles with the land-grabbing rulers of Europe and Asia. The mighty (?) *Ballard* Saint Germain should prevent this parceling out of his ancestral home.

As to the Count's death there are, as usual, conflicting stories. The Ballards say he never died, which belief has no doubt been based on statements made by some occult writers who make extraordinary claims as to his longevity.

If a manuscript attributed to him, *The Most Holy Trinosophia*, can be literally believed, his life ended by confinement in one of the dungeons of the Inquisition at Rome.   And if he was a member of the secret fraternity known as the Illuminati, as some believe, this kind of death seems plausible, for many of that Society were killed by the Inquisition.   Occultists, however, are inclined to interpret this MS. symbolically.

A church register at Eckernforde indicates that he died in 1784.   This is doubted by many, but the encyclopædias give credence to it and record that year as the time of his death.   The register reads as follows:

"Deceased on February 27th, buried on March 2nd, 1784, the so-called Comte de St. Germain and Weldon— further information not known—privately deposited in this church."

But like the "Wandering Jew" the Comte de St. Germain is still traditionally thought to be in existence.   By some he is supposed to be existing and working as the invisible power behind the throne in some of the nations of the world.   Even after his recorded death in 1784, he is thought to have done certain work among secret societies and Masonic orders.   He is supposed to have been one of the representatives of the French Masons at their convention at Paris in 1785, and to have done certain work preceding the French Revolution of 1789.   Thus in death as well as in life and birth, the same mystery about this man still eludes and baffles investigators.

There is a tendency for persons to let their imagination and fancy run riot in their efforts to make a greater mystery out of this man than the facts justify.   Some say he was Rasputin, the "Mad Monk of Russia," who is supposed to have brought about the downfall of the reign of the Czars, just as he is said to have had something to do with seeking to prevent or to encourage the French Revolution.   By still others he is thought to have had a previous existence as Christian Rosenkreuz, who founded certain of the Rosicrucian societies and secret orders during the

Middle Ages. And so on—with consistent mysteriousness.

That equally mysterious personage, the Russian noble-woman, Madame Helena Petrovna Blavatsky, who found-ed the Theosophical Society, calls him "the greatest Orien-tal Adept Europe has seen during the last centuries." *(Theosophical Glossary)*

Her occult brother and co-worker, Col. Henry S. Ol-cott, considered him "a messenger and agent of the White Lodge," using this term to mean "that Brotherhood of Adepts who stay back of the scenes and manipulate world affairs through agents for the good of humanity."

Lord Bulwer-Lytton, it is stated, wrote his famous occult novel, "Zanoni," around the character of Comte de St. Germain, and connected him with the French Revolu-tion.   Other writers have done likewise.

Manly P. Hall, of Los Angeles, and Mrs. Cooper-Oak-ley, of London, have both done considerable research in connection with Comte de St. Germain, to whose works the interested reader is referred for additional information. Hall states that over this character "hangs the veil of im-penetrable mystery."

Mrs. Cooper-Oakley shows that he was an associate and friend of Franz Anton Mesmer, and that they studied animal magnetism together. She quotes an Austrian writer as saying:

"In the Masonic and Rosicrucian literature one often finds hints as to the relations of St. Germain to the secret societies of Austria . . . He was addicted to alchemy, be-lieved in universal medicine and made studies as to animal magnetism . . . He belongs to the picture of 'Old Vienna' with its social mysteriousness; where it was swarming with Rosicrucians, Asiatics, Illuminates, Alchemists, Magneto-paths, Thaumaturgs, Templars, who all of them had many and willing adherents.

"Dr. Mesmer who knew the Comte St. Germain well from his stay in Paris, requested him to come to Vienna in order that he might pursue his study of animal magnetism with him.   St. Germain stayed secretly here . . . Dr. Mesmer was much helped by the Count . . . In Vienna St. Germain came in touch with many mystagogues. He visited the famous laboratory of the Rosicrucians in the Landstrasse . . . where he instructed for some time his brethren in the sciences of Solomon.   The Landstrasse, situated on the outskirts of Vienna, was for many centuries a region of spooks . . . The arrival of the Count (in 1735) created a great sensation in the initiated circles." *(The Comte de St. Germain,* by Mrs. Cooper-Oakley—pp. 157-9.)

Perhaps the real truth about this man lies between two extremes.   Considering the superstition of that day, the wise and cautious student will be inclined to discount the so-called magic of Comte de St. Germain's work.   He was undoubtedly learned and clever far beyond even the enlightened of that period.   Perhaps even, he took advantage of the credulity and ignorance of the age. It is conceivable that he even got a certain enjoyment out of telling mysterious tales, such as living at the time of Christ, possessing the wand of Moses, and having been on speaking terms with Melchizedek and other traditional characters—if we can believe the stories told of him. The Baron Munchausen type of mind is not confined to any age.

It is, however, most likely the Count was playing a certain part, for what exact purpose we know not.   The people of that age wanted mystery and marvels, as they do today.   Perhaps he fed them what they wanted in the way of wonders in order to achieve certain *political* ends. It is on this basis, no doubt, that we can most intelligently judge the work of the Comte de St. Germain, "Mystery Man" of the 18th century.

CHAPTER 13

THE BARD OF AVON GOES "I AM"

Shakespeare, the world's most illustrious author, in his latter celestial days, according to reports, has turned to the "Mighty I AM" for solace and comfort and has gotten sort of childish in his English.

The Bard who in his prime turned out from his gigantic literary mill the most astounding array of comedies, tragedies, and histories the world has ever seen, has, in these latter days, come solidly over to the Ballard banner and has published a book!

Formerly the most choice and creative in his use of words of any writer in the post-antediluvian world, he now confines himself to making simple and inane speeches over the "Light and Sound Ray," dotting the cosmic landscape with an over-use of such salutations as "Dear Hearts," "Beloved Ones," "Precious Students," and similar endearments to his happy family of I AM-ers. He has lost that extraordinary command of the English tongue which was undeniably his, turns frequently to American colloquialisms and slang, and is unbelievably careless in his efforts to get over to his "Beloved Students of Long Ago" the present aberrations of a former gigantic intellect.

The greatest of men, it seems, whether American, English, or Polynesian, have their weak moments when they go senile or from the other side of life try to speak to the children of earth. And if this effort at spirit communication be true in the use of the old-fashioned planchette or its modern revival, the Ouija board, what may we expect of the streamlined "Light and Sound Ray"?

It seems that the Ballards have communicated with the author of the Shakespearean plays over their marvelous Light and Sound Ray, and have revealed most startling information. In the most sober truth and in the most approved Munchausen fashion, they tell us that the author of the Shakespearean plays is none other than their own garrulous "Saint Germain"!

And herein lies another story just as marvelous, for evidently accepting the rather discredited idea that Lord Frances Bacon was the real author of the Shakespearean literature, they tell us in the same breath that Bacon was, and is, also their "Saint Germain"!

A search through the literature put out under the names of Shakespeare and Bacon, however, reveals no particular fondness in either case for the "Mighty I AM" of the Ballards. In fact, in neither case does it seem that the "I AM" has been mentioned at all—which seems strange considering "Saint Germain's" present ardor for the "I AM." If Saint Germain was Bacon, and he wrote the Shakespearean plays, why no mention of the "I AM" in the Baconian and Shakespearean literature? Why did Saint Germain at that time hide his "I AM" under a bushel, only to have it peep out in all its effulgence under the present dynasty of the Ballards?

The whole weird story of the strange reincarnations of "Saint Germain" is told in the Ballard article on that gentleman published on pages 5 to 9 of the March, 1936, *Voice of the I AM*, and therefore is strictly and unqualifiedly authentic to the last word.

In this article there is an earnest but considerably strained effort to link the name of William Shakespeare in some way with their "I AM." They say:

"The name, William Shakespeare, under which He wrote the plays, signifies that it was the *Will* of the *I AM* that He *shake* the *Spear* of Wisdom at the darkness of ignorance . . . " (p. 6.)

One may have to re-read this play on words to catch the point. We wonder if all folks who have William as their name are for the same reason "I AM-ers"? All they have to do to become so is to capitalize the "iam" which follows the "Will" part of the name—and it is done!

Yet the Ballards condemn the numerologists for doing capers with names and numbers!

Complicating the history of "Saint Germain" and Bacon still more, we read in the aforementioned article the following amazing statement:

"His [Saint Germain's] last embodiment was that of Lord Francis Bacon, *who was the son of Queen Elizabeth by her husband, Lord Leister . . .*"! (p. 5.)

Most odd when we remember that England's virgin Queen never had a husband—at least none that history records.

Also, Bacon, it seems, was the perfectly good son of Sir Nicholas Bacon and his legally-wed wife. And there was no "Lord Leister." Perhaps the Ballards referred to the court favorite, Lord Leicester, who also had a spouse.

That, unfortunately, isn't all of the affair. Mixing history and invention still further, we read:

"Saint Germain illumined and raised His body in 1684 . . . " (p. 7.)

Now, history records that Bacon died in *1626*. Therefore, if "Saint Germain" as "Bacon," raised his body in *1684*, he made his "Ascension" *fifty-eight years after his recorded death!*

In other words, "Saint Germain," miracle man that he is, "raised" his body from the grave after it had lain there in its dust and whitened bones for a half century and more!

Just another "I AM" miracle. Which brings up the startling thought that there is now a chance for the great grandparents of devoted I AM-ers to make their "Ascensions"—even though dead and buried for a century or so!

But going back still further into history, we discover further news about this remarkable "Saint Germain," news that should be of particular interest to Bible students.

We learn that this odd and quick-change character was also the *Prophet Samuel*—he it was who sent a thunderstorm against the Philistines and saved the day for the besieged Israelites. That, indeed, does in fact sound like the heroic Saint Germain. He has always been apt at throwing the "lightning" and that sort of thing.

But it is not recorded that Samuel knew anything about the "I AM" which seems odd, considering the fact that he today (as "Saint Germain"), talks constantly about it.

Besides, Samuel got *old*, which the ever-youthful "Saint Germain" is surely not supposed to do. For according to the Bible, after Samuel was dead, the Witch of Endor at the earnest entreaty of King Saul, brought him forth as a ghost from the realm of departed spirits. And Samuel came forth as an *"old man . . . covered with a robe,"* and prophesied. (I Sam. 28:14.)

That "old man" was the formerly youthful "'Master Saint Germain," who 70,000 years ago was "King of the Sahara Desert," the one who "looked like a God" in his "golden hair that hung to his shoulders." (p. 151, U. M.)

Such, it seems, are the rigors of Time, which "Masters" as well as men cannot remove or affect.

But this composite Saint Germain-Bacon-Shakespeare-Samuel-King-of-the-Sahara character has still further destiny to fulfill, even though a somewhat symbolic and static one. He is in addition to all this none other than our own revered *"Uncle Sam"!* He is called that, says Mrs. Ballard, because "Saint Germain" is in charge of America and was the Prophet *SAM*-uel!

Just how the "Uncle" part has come in, she never has said. But as the I AM-ers have their "Daddy" and "Mamma" Ballard—why not an *"Uncle"* Saint Germain!

It must be evident from all of this that the Comte de

St. Germain of the 18th century cannot on any basis of fact and reason be the strange, pieced-together creation which the Ballards call their "Ascended Master Saint Germain."

If, as they admit, the Comte de St. Germain of the 18th century was an *"Ascended Master"* when he lived in the apartment at the chateau provided for him by Louis XV and talked to a multitude of different people and did all the other *physical* things attributed to him—why doesn't he do similar physical things today? Why doesn't he show himself to other human beings besides members of the Ballard family?

No, he does none of these things. He hides out in so-called mystic retreats, where no one can see him. He takes astral excursions instead of the ferry or coach. He visits only the Ballards, coming in through the wall or window of their hotel room, and goes out perhaps by the roof. He hovers over the Ballards on the platform like a wraith, and speaks the most inane things, far different than he spoke when he was just an *un*-Ascended being—Lord Bacon—and assertedly wrote the plays of William Shakespeare!

If the Ballard "Ascension" can do that much for a scholar and a great man, what might not it do for us?

We shall have to, therefore, on the clear basis of reason, separate the historical Comte de St. Germain from the Ballard creation of that name, and we have nothing left then but a phantasmagoria of the Ballard mind, or, if you believe in such things, a spook or an astral wraith.

Yet, this wraith, spook, phantom, thought-image, or whatever you want to call it, functions as a *"PSYCHIC DICTATOR"* over the minds and actions of hundreds of thousands of otherwise good and patriotic Americans!

It (or he) tells them what to eat, what to wear, and what not to. It flatters them on occasions, and threatens them generally all the time. It tells them when they can "Ascend" and when they can't. It tells them what

"Friends" to place at the seat of the United States Government, and what will happen to some already there.

It is the strangest sort of dictatorship extant in a world already encompassed with odd dictatorships. It is a dictatorship which is not backed by a police force or army, or by a physical-plane Hitler, Stalin, or Mussolini, but by the *psychically*-armed might of the Ballard legions of "Ascended Masters" that are pledged to sweep America and the earth.

And their people *believe* it—and have for five years!

CHAPTER 14

DOCUMENTARY EVIDENCE OF PLAGIARISM

Whence have come all of Guy Ballard's fantastic voyages to foreign lands, his hobnobbing with mighty "Masters" in caves and retreats? Did he get them out of his own fertile imagination as legitimate story writers do, or did he, perforce, get them from the literary creations of others? Or did somebody else write them for him?

To begin with, it may be said there is always a certain amount of unconscious appropriating. Authors are amazed and chagrined sometimes to discover that they have unintentionally used words, expressions, and even incidents which they thought were original with them but which came from the works of other authors. If any author does that, the other may charitably forgive, for he knows not when he himself may fall into such a ditch.

Then there is the legitimate making use of another's work, by giving due credit to the one from whom the author borrows. And here again most authors are usually generous, providing too much is not taken so as to devalue their own work.

Lastly, there is the direct steal from a book, putting it out as the author's own. That is dyed-in-the-wool plagiarism, a literary crime of the first water.

In the first division, Ballard or his collaborator may have *unconsciously* used some ideas from others, and for this they may be forgiven. In the second division, they are manifestly *not* the type of authors who would acknowledge using the works of another.

Are they then guilty of this last and most flagrant

literary crime—the *consciously* planned, premeditated steal from somebody else?   In other words, have they plagiarized?

We submit the following evidence to literary critics, to copyright attorneys, and to Ballard students who believe that Godfre Ray King's experiences are really his own and his teachings from "Ascended Masters."

In a book entitled *A Dweller on Two Planets*, published by the Poseid Publishing Co., Los Angeles, there is an account of an experience almost identical with that which has been later recorded by Godfre Ray King in his book *Unveiled Mysteries*.

Phylos, the hero of the first book, meets his "Master" on a mountain in California, just as Godfre does.   And Phylos and his Master visit together a marvelous retreat, as do Godfre and *his* Master.   Both retreats are hollowed out of the solid rock of a mountain.   Quong is the name of Phylos' teacher, and his retreat is at Mt. Shasta, California.   Saint Germain's retreat is at Grand Teton mountain in Wyoming.

Now, note the deadly parallelism in the two columns given below:

COMPARE THE TWO ACCOUNTS

PHYLOS, THE THIBETAN	BALLARD, THE MESSENGER
Time: 1894	Time: 1930
Place: A cave in a mountain, *Mt. Shasta, Calif.*	Place: A cave in a mountain, *Grand Teton, Wyoming.*
Incident: Phylos, neophyte in the Mysteries, visits an occult retreat with his "Master."	Incident: Ballard, neophyte in the Mysteries, visits an occult retreat with his "Ascended Master."
. . . We halted in front of a HUGE ledge of basaltic *rocks* . . . (p. 270) The ledge was broken and twisted AS IF	Going to a point where HUGE masses of *stone* . . . (p. 76) . . . Masses of stone lay in *confusion,* AS IF

by some rending
convulsion. (p. 270)
Against the cliff rested a
GIANT block . . .
(p. 270)
. . . He [Quong] TOUCHED
the **enormous** quadrangular
block. (p. 271)
Immediately it
TIPPED on edge . . . (p. 271)
He SWUNG back the
door-stone . . . (p. 272)
He . . . STEPPED within the
tunnel . . . I followed. (p. 272)
. . . The *passage*
LED into the mountain.
(p. 273)
After going about
TWO HUNDRED FEET . . .
(p. 273)
. . . We came to a DOOR made
apparently of BRONZE . . .
(p. 273)
This door gave entrance to a
large CIRCULAR CHAMBER. .
(p. 273)
With DOMELIKE CEILING
ten or a dozen feet high at
its junction with the wall
(p. 273)
. . . All about me shone a
marvelous WHITE LIGHT . . .
The same wonderful illumina-
tion was **omnipresent** . . .
(p. 273)

giants had hurled them in a
war upon each other. (p. 76)
. . . As if
GIANTS had hurled them . . .
(p. 76)
. . . Saint Germain TOUCHED
a *great boulder.*
(p. 76)
Instantly, the **enormous** mass
TIPPED OUT . . . (p. 76)
The great mass of bronze . . .
SWUNG slowly open. . . (p.76)
He STEPPED forward . . .
admitted us. (p. 76)
. . . A *stairway* cut in the
solid rock LED downward.
(p. 76)
We descended some
TWO HUNDRED FEET . . .
(p. 76)
. . . We . . . stood before a
large BRONZE DOOR.
(p. 76)
We . . . entered another
SPACE CIRCULAR in shape.
(p. 76)
The ARCHED CEILING rising
some ten feet higher than
the side-walls . . .
(p. 82)
A soft WHITE LIGHT, which
Saint Germain explained
was an **omnipresent** force . . .
flooded the entire place.
(p. 81)

Compare the italics, capitals, and bold-face type in one column with those in the other. Can anything be more revealing than the *real* source of Ballard's alleged "true" experiences with Saint Germain at the retreat in the Grand Teton mountain?

Forty-six years apart in time, a thousand miles apart in space—yet the *same incident* told virtually in the same words and phraseology, or with synonyms that mean practically the same thing!

Literary critics, copyright experts, and even their poor duped followers must agree that if this be coincidence, then Ballard is the most coincidental person on the face of the earth. The fact-finding Ripley ought to put it in his "Believe-It-or-Not" column.

What is one to think of a man who swears on the platform by all that is holy, that every word in "those blessed books" is true? A man who says over and over again that his books represent actually his own *personal experiences?*

The parallelism given here is no rare and isolated evidence of Ballard plagiarism. Such a thing occurs frequently in their first two books. We have space only for a few additional examples.

Does not the one given below show even the possible source of the Ballard "Saint Germain"?

Back in 1894 Will L. Garver's book, entitled *The Brother of the Third Degree,* came forth as one of the popular occult novels of the day. In it the mysterious Comte de St. Germain was featured, just as he was later featured in the Ballard books.

In the Garver book the Comte de St. Germain is represented as having powerful political influence, secretly working with Napoleon I., Emperor of France, to bring about a United States of Europe. The hero of the story, Alphonso, is a *"government agent."*

In the Ballard book, of course, the Comte de St. Germain is likewise pictured as having powerful political influence, but is working mainly with the United States of America instead of Europe. The hero, Godfre Ray King (Guy Ballard), is represented as being on *"government business."*

Compare now how the heroes of both stories describe

their contacts with the same Comte de St. Germain. Note how both travel *astrally* with him:

THE GARVER BOOK	THE BALLARD BOOK
He [St. Germain] was tall and sparely built, with *long* GOLDEN HAIR and a light curly, chestnut beard. (p. 290)	. . . Saint Germain stood before us . . . His beautiful GOLDEN HAIR *hung to his shoulders.* (p. 151)
His eyes were BLUE and shone with a *fiery* luster . . . *Face not marked by a single wrinkle* . . . (p. 290)	The *piercing,* sparkling VIOLET of his eyes . . . *His features were very regular* . . . (p. 151)
Suddenly a VOICE commanded me to COME with him . . . (p. 353)	. . . I heard his VOICE say distinctly: "COME!" (p. 128)
Without question or even surprise, I OBEYED, and felt myself going through SPACE with the *rapidity* of thought. (p. 353)	I had learned to OBEY that call, and . . . passed *quickly* through SPACE . . . (p. 128)

In the Garver book there are many other parallels which could have been given, but we must pass on very briefly to quotations from other books.

The Prince of Atlantis by Lillian Elizabeth Roy, published by The Educational Press, New York, in 1929, contains many similar scenes and incidents which later were recorded in Ballard's *Unveiled Mysteries.*

In both books there is the same "Great Luminous Being," who comes to warn the people of an impending cataclysm which would strike unless the people heeded the warning, obeyed the "Law of the One," and recognized their "Source."

There is the same great conclave of people, a great "banquet," the wise and good "Emperor" and his "golden-haired children," the same division into two classes of people, and the "Voice" of the great "Cosmic Being" which sounds out a warning to the disobedient people telling them of the coming cataclysm.

In both books the people are given a certain time limit in which to heed the warning—"Seven weeks" in one book, "Seven days" in the other. But all to no avail.

The cataclysm comes, and the "wicked" perish in the ensuing deluge. In both books the "Emperor's children" and the "Children of Light" miraculously escape.

The three current Ballards, as might be expected, were the Emperor's "golden-haired children" of that ancient civilization of seventy thousand years ago. A great "Cosmic Master" came, just in time, and withdrew them into the "Golden Etheric City of Light."

In the occult novel, *Myriam and the Mystic Brotherhood,* by Maude Lesseuer Howard, published nearly two decades ago, there are many incidents and characters which Ballard similarly tells about, including mystic caves which had been "hollowed out of solid rock" of the mountain. There are "Initiations," golden-robed "Masters," various "Ascensions," and some very young "Children of the Light" who take part in all these mysteries.

In Baird T. Spalding's series of books, *Life and Teaching of the Masters of the Far East*—the first two published over ten years before the Ballard books—we likewise find many similarities. There is much about the "I AM," the "Ascension," messages from great "Masters," dazzling "Light Rays," precipitated meals—and even gold coins snapped right out of the atmosphere!

Edna Ballard, at some of her very early private classes in Chicago—a few years before the publication of *Unveiled Mysteries*—read frequently from the Spalding books. Spalding himself spent some weeks as a guest at the Ballard home. She also read other occult literature to this class, including, as stated before, the Pelley magazines. Mr. Ballard who had *secretly* returned to Chicago after his alleged experience with "Saint Germain" on Mt.

Shasta was only occasionally at these early classes and was spoken of very mysteriously. He kept himself very much in the background—for reasons which will in a couple of chapters be clear.

Then after some months of reading from Pelley, Spalding, and other literature, Edna Ballard began to read from a series of so-called "Discourses." She was very mysterious about them, and said she could not tell where they came from, as she had no "permission."

Later, however, she stated these discourses had come direct to her and Mr. Ballard over a *"Light and Sound Ray* at their home on 84th Place. They were at that time written on thin paper and were full of corrections and interpolations, showing that whoever was responsible for them had changed his or her mind frequently.

These "Discourses" were the originals which later formed the basis for the Ballard publication, *The "I AM" Discourses*. There is no doubt but that Edna Ballard took the utmost liberty in freely "editing" these discourses which were supposed to have been given by great "Perfect Beings" over the marvelous "Light and Sound Ray"—allegedly something *new* in the history of the world.

But, alas! this "Light and Sound Ray" is found in all its marvelousness in Marie Corelli's occult novel, *The Secret Power*, published in 1921. Which proves again there is nothing new under the sun—not even the Ballard "Light and Sound Ray"!

It would perhaps be boring to some readers to quote in detail all the various selections from books which undoubtedly formed the basis for much of the Ballard work. Those who want to investigate further along this line are referred to the author's series of five brochures, particularly numbers 4 and 5, entitled *The Source of the Ballard Writings* and *The Ballard Saint Germain*. (Truth Research Publications, Los Angeles.)

It is interesting and surprising to note one odd thing.

The first Ballard book, *Unveiled Mysteries,* is supposed to be the first of a series of instructions on the "Mighty I AM." Yet in this book—which tells all about Ballard's contact with Saint Germain—there is no mention whatever of the "Mighty I AM."

The "*Magic Presence,*" however, which was their second book, abounds in this expression of the "Mighty I AM."

Now, why didn't Saint Germain mention these "magic words" to Ballard on Mt. Shasta in 1930 instead of waiting two years to speak them over the marvelous "Light and Sound Ray" in his home in Chicago?

The evidence points to the fact that *Edna Ballard* had a good deal to do with injecting into the work the name of "Mighty I AM," as well as being responsible for much else in "those blessed books."

It is reliably stated by a party who was staying at the Ballard home that while Edna Ballard worked on the MSS. of those marvelous "Ascended Master" books, Guy Ballard washed and hung up clothes!

Their former Assoociate Director, who traveled with them during part of the time that the MS. for *The Magic Presence* was in preparation, writes:

"I think Mrs. Ballard did most of the work. In fact, so far as I could see while I was with them, *she* was the boss, and he did just what she told him to do. She also was in full charge of *The Magic Presence,* which was in preparation while I was with them . . . She spent much time working on this MS. the whole time I was with them."

Indeed, in the early days in Chicago it is stated that Mrs. Ballard seemed sometimes to be more conversant with those marvelous experiences of Godfre Ray King than Guy Ballard himself! People who attended those early classes say that it was she who generally answered questions in regard to those experiences. Later, however, it seems, that he became more familiar with his own experiences and would swear to their truth with the greatest of intensity.

We are also told by those who were in close association with the Ballards that when they first came to Los Angeles in the Spring of 1935—shortly after they had gotten off the MS. of *The Magic Presence* to the commercial printers in Chicago—Mrs. Ballard had something like a *"trunk-load of books with her."*

Just why was the need for Mrs. Ballard to cart those old books around with her? Books that had been outdated and outmoded by the marvelous *new* teachings of the Ascended Masters! Books they later advised their people *not* to read!

We pass now to another little irregularity in literary acknowledgment.

When the two Accredited Messengers of Saint Germain arrived in Los Angeles on their first sweep of the country—she with her books and he with his Arabian Nights' tales—they told the story of how Godfre Ray King had visited the Ascended Masters in their secret retreats, had dined and talked with them, had slept in their households, had bathed in their "circular Roman baths," all perfumed divinely with "scent of roses." (p. 70, M. P.)

Then one happy day Mrs. Ballard announced to a thrilled and expectant Los Angeles audience that on a certain afternoon and evening they would show actual pictures of these magnificent Beings.

The day at last arrived, and the writer was on hand to see those marvelous pictures.

He had never seen a picture of an *"Ascended"* Master. He had, however, seen pictures of regular Masters—at least he was informed they were Masters through his reading of theosophical and other occult literature, and he was just a bit curious to see how an "Ascended" Master differed from those of the regular kind.

Well, imagine his surprise when he saw staring back at

him from the stereopticon screen those same *"un*-Ascended" Masters he had seen years before in theosophical books —but now all tinted up with dashes of water color here and there!

He naturally listened for an acknowledgment of debt to the Theosophical Society for the privilege of showing these pictures; but, none came!

These great and magnificent "Ascended-Master" pictures were shown time and again as *their own*, with no acknowledgment whatsoever as to their real source; and balls of "Blue Lightning" were thrown at any "vicious" individual or organization that dared call attention to this and other little irregularities.

In that early day, the Mighty I AM movement sprouted so rapidly that its Accredited Messengers had to present much that was secondhand, and this included not only water-colored pictures of Theosophical Masters but even a couple of the Masters themselves! They reported that the two Theosophical Masters who had started that Society (the Master M. and K. H.) had come over to the Mighty I AM banner and were now "*Ascended* Masters"!

For the good Ballard student who might feel inclined to doubt that the Accredited Messengers of the Ascended Masters would pawn off on him, as it were, pictures of *un*-Ascended beings, when he has been trained for years to worship "Ascended" ones, we refer him to the Theosophical book, *Through the Eyes of the Masters*, by David Anrias, published in 1932 by George Routledge & Sons, Ltd., London, where he will see what undoubtedly are the self-same "Ascended Masters" which were shown many times on the Ballard stereopticon screen.

Furthermore, Mrs. Ballard in giving her verbal descriptions of these Masters repeated almost verbatim what Anrias had said about them—and for variety added some of the descriptions of Annie Besant and Charles Leadbeater, well-known Theosophical writers on such subjects.

The "Ascended Masters" having come to life on the screen instead of in *person* as promised, the divinely-appointed Messengers proceeded to show weird-looking "Thought Forms" of persons in love, in hate, and afflicted with green-eyed jealousy.

These pictures bore every indication of having been taken from a Theosophical book by Besant and Leadbeater entitled *Thought Forms,* first published in 1905; but so far as the uninformed in the audience knew, they were fresh from the Ballard astral picture gallery!

Then the Accredited Messengers of the Ascended Masters showed gorgeously-colored plates of great "Cosmic Forces and Beings."

But once again the heavenly exhibit had its earthly counterpart. In a book, entitled *Watchers of the Seven Spheres,* by H. K. Challoner, published by E. P. Dutton & Co., Inc., New York, in 1935, we find these self-same gorgeously-colored plates of great Cosmic Forces and Beings. Furthermore, Mrs. Ballard utilized the descriptive material in this book in explaining the status and function of those Cosmic Beings—but of course without acknowledgment.

When the dust of illusion which has thrown itself over this movement has sufficiently settled, we wonder whether this cult of "Saint Germain" will not go down in metaphysical history as the greatest "occult steal" of many centuries—if not of all time.

CHAPTER 15

THE "MASTER" BOOK-SELLING RACKET

For five years a "Master" book-selling racket has been under way in America. No other series of books in the history of America has had such astonishing claims made for them.

"In those precious books there are no human concepts or opinions . . . They contain the answer to anything and everything . . . Never was there such a thing written on earth . . . They will remain the glory of the land for hundreds of years."

And so on in ever-increasing hyperbolic utterances, all to be quoted accurately from the Ballard literature.

The Ballard flare for hyperbole is most manifest in their efforts to *sell* these books. To this end they brought forth mighty "Masters." They had great "Cosmic Beings" institute sales campaigns. They said the covers of those "marvelous books," as seen from the "Ascended Master's Octave Light," were made of "precious jewels." That each successive book of the series was "more magnificent" than the first—a veritable "stairway" to the blessed students' "glorious freedom."

And there are still more blessings to be dispensed to the proud possessor of those priceless books:

Through a special process, known only to the "Ascended Masters, mighty *"Cosmic Radiations"* exude from each book. These "Radiations" are charged into the books some time during their manufacture or sale. Mighty Ascended Masters come forth from cosmic space to attend to this. They sweep through the four walls of the commercial print shop where these books are manufactured. They invade the so-called "Saint Germain Press." They enter the I AM Temples where these books are sold. All for the purpose of charging their "Ascended Master Radiations" into these books, for no book is complete without it!

In addition to this, the great Saint Germain himself gives a very *special* Radiation at the time his senior Messenger autographs any of the books. This is as it should be. The sale has been made; the cash is in the "I AM" strong box—or, as the saying is, "sent back into the work"; and the fortunate student has the book.

This is the way it is done: A crowd forms in the lobby for the special ceremony of having one or more of those precious books autographed. They must be *new* ones—freshly purchased. The old ones are refused an autograph.

Guy Ballard, chief autographer, sits serenely at his desk. Surrounding him is his bodyguard of "Minute Men," whose job it is to keep process servers and other "vicious" individuals away. Saint Germain, chief "charger," stands at Ballard's right elbow. The voltage for each book is never stated, but is said to be high. The current flows down Ballard's right arm and into his autographing fingers. Then somehow it spreads out into the book—which is never the same afterwards.

The book has, of course, as we have said, been charged at the factory, but this "special" charge given cooperatively by the Germain-Ballard combination is different. It is "transcendent." So much so, that Saint Germain is never absent when this autographing ceremony is to be performed. European matters wait. Important conferences at Washington hold their fire. The important thing is the autographing and "charging" of those precious books. Charge accounts, however, are not accepted. The terms are *cash*. It is sufficient to "charge" the books!

On occasions, "St. Germain" as chief electric-charger for the Ballard organization, is ably assisted by "Lady

Ascended Masters."

When the latest of the large bound books came out, the *"Goddess of Purity"* came forth to celebrate the occasion and stimulate book sales. She made her own announcement (through Mr. Ballard of course) on the stage of the Shrine Auditorium in Los Angeles on January 1, 1939—a sort of New Years gift to prospective buyers of the new Ballard opus.

"Henceforth," she said, "I shall join your Beloved Saint Germain in charging My Purity into every book that the Messenger autographs." (p. 8, Feb., 1939, v.)

She urged the fortunate purchasers to "place the books out of handling of others," for the reason that these individually-charged Radiations should not be mixed with the lower-octave emanations from other people. Each I AM student is urged to buy and keep an individual set of books for his own personal use and not lend them to others—a beautiful system of increasing book sales!

Five of their regularly bound books sell at $2.50 to $3.00 each, the total amounting to $13.75. Each student is urged to buy *all* these books by the great Saint Germain himself.

"If you have not the FULL SET of those books," says this book-selling Ascended Master, "do not let another thirty days go over your head before you have them." (p. 2, Sept. 20, 1938, G. L.)

The Ballards claim "over one million earnest students." Therefore, if they can psychologize these students sufficiently to have a million of them buy a full set of books, there will flow into the Ballard strong box to be "used in the work" the startling sum of *Thirteen Million, Seven Hundred Fifty Thousand good American dollars!*

Their students make supreme efforts to own these books, and pathetic stories have come to the writer of sacrifices made to purchase them, some going without material food for days in order to secure the "spiritual" sustenance supposed to be contained in them.

Then there is the Ballard monthly magazine, *The Voice of the I AM,* which also must net them quite a tidy sum of money. The subscription rate is $3.00 per year, or 35c per copy. When the first issue came out in February, 1936, they also brought forth "Jesus" (!) to boost its circulation.

"We shall endeavor to make the *Voice of the I AM,*" says this false Christ, "the most sought after periodical of the day . . . It is My wish and that of the Host of Ascended Masters that all students of the I AM firmly decree this . . ." (p. 9, Feb., 1936, v.)

The result was a "Circulation Decree," which the poor students shouted and shouted until they were hoarse:

"We decree that the circulation of the magazine, *The Voice of the I AM,* exceed ONE MILLION subscribers in 1937!"

Then there is in addition to this a miscellaneous lot of other articles of Ascended Master merchandise to be sold at good prices over the counter in the various I AM Temples scattered throughout the nation. There are pins, rings, emblems, bookmarks, seals, folders, flags, booklets, trinkets. There are songs, phonograph records, and transcription rentals.

Songs—and there are many of them—sell for $1.00. Phonograph records—and there have been dozens—bring $2.50. "I AM" pins sell at $1.00. I AM rings command $12.00. Books for the blind $5.25 to $7.75 each, or $26.75 for the set of four. Jesus' picture sells for $2.00 and up; likewise the bearded Saint Germain. "*The Old Man of the Hills*" brings $2.25 postpaid; and large pictures of the Beloved Messenger, Guy W. Ballard, are tops at $25.00 each, express collect.

A small "Chart of the Presence" sells at $1.00; a larger one for $15.00; and their de luxe chart a bargain at $200.00! Their "Violet Consuming Flame" another bargain at $200.00! But express extra, and no discount to dealers and group leaders!

The brain grows weary in computing the possible income which might result from these articles of Ascended Master merchandise sold in I AM Temples and spread among "one million earnest students."

The Ballard radio broadcasts are not only paid for almost exclusively by the students, but they also have to rent Mrs. Ballard's transcription records at $20.00 per record, cash in advance.

"Money cannot be spent in any better manner," says the great God Himalaya, who came all the way from India to say it, and adds: "There is no thing in the world which would render such transcendent blessing as money used in the broadcasting of the 'I AM' to the world." (p. 311, A. M. L.)

The hard-pressed students do their best to meet the demands of these "Master" salesmen, as will be seen from the following notice which was passed out at one of the I AM Temples in New York:

"Word has been received that Mrs. Ballard would like at least seven nights (ten, if possible) over WMCA Broadcasting Station. The cost is about $185 a night. The Great Arcturus said that the blessing of those who make possible the broadcasting of this Mighty Truth shall know no bounds."

Naturally, to secure Great Arcturus' blessing, the students got busy at once to secure the $1850.00. An appropriate decree was selected, and the students began to work on getting this money with a vengeance. An informant writes:

"This decree was given in unison at all the meetings in New York, Connecticut, and New Jersey, and repeated at the meeting I attended *thirty times,* until toward the end the whole crowd was shouting and indeed some of the women were screaming it, bordering on hysteria."

CHAPTER 16

WHERE THE MONEY GOES

Having shown in the last chapter the tremendous money possibilities of a "Master" merchandising racket, it might be well to inquire: "Where does all the money go?"

"It all goes back to the Work," shouted Guy Ballard many times from the platform, while his good wife always expressed quick agreement.

But to make doubly sure that their students really appreciate this great sacrifice of having their hard-earned money go back to the "Work," and no doubt to squelch nasty little rumors to the contrary, they have their ever-ready "Ascended Masters" come forth to back them up.

"Every dollar that comes in from their books," says no less a personage than John the Beloved, "they put into This Work to save mankind and America." (p. 13, Feb., 1938, v.)

Another so-called Ascended Master, who happens to be the white-haired old man who allegedly made his Ascension off of Mt. Shasta after Ballard gave him a "Crystal Cup," is naturally a good booster for Guy Ballard and all his works.

"Precious ones," says this formerly white-haired old man, "do not let the silly human reports go forth which have been spread at times, that they [the Messengers] are flourishing with money. All they have is the Love Gifts of the students to carry on the work. Not so long ago, the report went forth that they had plenty of money. The Love Gifts from that class did not take care of the express on their trunks, but they never complain." (p. 217, A. M. D.)

In view of the fact that one of their former staff members reports that 4500 pounds of expressage (28 trunks) went forward to the east from their Los Angeles class in January, 1939, it is little to be wondered at that their self-sacrificing students have difficulty keeping sufficient "Love Gifts" going their way to pay the expressage on all this opulence, or to put them up at the most expensive hotels.

Still, these poor students do what they can; and in addition to making themselves poorer and poorer in efforts to support "The Work," they use up their energies in shouting long decrees trying to induce the Cosmos to unload its wealth to the Ballards personally. We quote, in part, one of these decrees:

"Mighty I AM Presence, Thou Great Treasure House of the Universe, I don't look to channels, I look to YOU as you are my source of supply for everything! ... Release, this hour, to our *Blessed Mommie* and *Daddy Ballard,* to all the sincere I AM students everywhere, and to me, ONE MILLION DOLLARS in cash money! TAX FREE! ... I thank Thee, Thou dost always answer my every call instantly, infinitely, eternally, and visible and tangibly manifest in my hands and use."

It is *not* stated that this "One Million Dollars" for Blessed Mommie and Daddy Ballard is to go "back into the Work." The intention is that it is to go to the Ballards personally.

These people say that they "love America" and shout decrees supporting the flag and the Constitution—yet they don't want their country to have a cent of tax money! Nor do they include the Government in this "million dollar" shower from the Cosmos! It is all to go to Me and Mine!

Despite the Ballards' public profession of not wanting anything for themselves, the above decree—asking a cool million for Blessed Mommie and Daddy Ballard—shows that the situation is quite different. Students are not permitted to make up their own decrees. All decrees must originate from the Ballard headquarters—and presiding over the decree-making department is Edna Ballard herself!

The author has in his possession some very revealing private letters written by the Ballards, showing that of all people these Messengers of business-like "Ascended Masters" are most desirous of possessing money for *themselves*.

These letters were written and signed by one or both of the Ballards, and were addressed to their former "Associate Director." In them appear many references about money matters, book sales, and some real "Ascended-Master" concern over cutting down on percentage discounts given to book stores. We have space for only one of these letters. It was written by Guy Ballard, and signed "George" as that was the name the alleged reincarnated Washington frequently used in corresponding with his Associate Director.

New York City, N. Y.
December 18, 1934.

My Dear ————:

We cannot give anyone 50% and have anything left for *ourselves,* and furthermore, we are not going to do it . . .

Saint Germain said in the beginning that 30 and 33⅓ was the limit to be given anyone . . .

Saint Germain said that he wanted us to have $1.00 per copy clear on all books as *his gift to us.*

I am the channel that has made all this possible and I do not intend to be swallowed up by this terrible commercial thing that has always forgotten the originator of a thing from which others have received MILLIONS.

(Signed) GEORGE

We fail to see in this letter any mention made of this "Saint Germain Dollar" going "back into the Work." Three months before, when the Ballards were working on this man trying to get him to promote their movement, they wrote him: "*We no longer possess anything so far as our personalities are concerned*"! Yet, how different are their later letters to him! They even had in mind millions!

As further proof that all the money does *not* go back into the work, we now quote from a deposition made by Mrs. Ballard, dated April 11, 1940, at Los Angeles, in the Superior Court of the State of California. She was called as a witness to testify in a divorce suit against her son, Donald Ballard. The questions below are by plaintiff's lawyer; answers are by Mrs. Ballard.

Q. Now, the furniture that they have in your home, whose property is that, do you know?

A. That is mine.

Q. Your property?

A. Yes, sir.

Q. Individually?

A. Bought in Mr. Ballard's and my own names, I have all the bills to show for it.

Q. That wasn't bought in the account of the St. Germain Foundation?

A. No.

Q. And did you make a gift of that to them?

A. I did not.

Q. To Donald alone?

A. It was to Donald alone, only until such time as we again had our own permanent home. We loaned them the use of those things until our own personal home was established here.

Here we have a statement made by Mrs. Ballard, on oath, that it was *she* who owned the furniture ($7,000 worth) in her son's home, and that she and Mr. Ballard were planning to have their own permanent home in Los Angeles.

These statements are contrary to the Ballards' statements made on the publc platform to the effect that they owned *nothing* in the way of a home and never expected to, that the nearest to a home they would get would be "Donald's and Marjorie's home."

After admitting that she was *"Treasurer"* of the Saint Germain Foundation and head of the Saint Germain Press, Mrs. Ballard was asked the following questions:

Q. What assets does the St. Germain Foundation have?
A. Well, I couldn't tell you that.
Q. Do you have any idea?
A. No.
Q. You couldn't give us an approximate estimate?
A. No, I couldn't?
Q. Could you on the St. Germain Press?
A. No, I couldn't, I am not familiar with that.

Most *remarkable* answers for the "Treasurer" and head of a big merchandising business!

Perhaps only an income tax man from the Department of Internal Revenue will be able to figure out where the money goes—but of course their "Tax Free" decree works against it!

CHAPTER 17

SOME ANTECEDENT HISTORY

Seventy thousand years ago, according to that modern Arabian Nights' Entertainment, *Unveiled Mysteries,* a certain king of the Sahara Desert had three beautiful children. This king was a good king, not wicked as kings of fairy tales are wont to be. He ruled wisely and well, and was looked upon almost as a God by his adoring subjects. His children were adorable, two manly boys and a lovely girl, and they had golden hair and violet eyes. The sons wore form-fitting garments made of metallic gold, with breast-plates like a great sun of jewels. They wore sandals set with precious stones. The daughter, a vision of loveliness, appeared among the courtiers and gallants of that day attired in golden garments covered with diamonds which glittered with every movement of her body. Her hair was like spun gold, and it hung almost to the floor. There was no wicked stepmother to mar the peace and tranquility of this happy royal family.

In this picture of the ancient civilization of the Sahara Desert we secure our first introduction to the "Ascended Master Saint Germain," who was a mighty king in those days.

And his three lovely children are none other than the three current Ballards—*Lotus, Godfre,* and *Donald!*

In a later civilization Ballard and son Donald become priests of an ancient temple in Egypt, and Lotus its fair vestal virgin.

Still later, the golden-haired, blue-eyed Donald is crowned king over the red-skinned, dark-eyed Incas in an ancient civilization of fourteen thousand years ago, and all was happy, too, in this forgotten kingdom of so long ago.

But alas! the scene changes, the years move on, and in present days of worldly strife, kings do not rule so wisely and well, nor do vestal virgins tend so faithfully the glowing altar fires.

And so as the curtain rises on this latest scene of all, we discover the former Emperor's golden-haired children, the three Ballards, in the not-so-exotic, bustling city of Chicago bearing no imprint or badge of royalty.

Just like other mortals who have outlived somehow the fairy tales of childhood, they have their disappointments and their struggles. There was no king or prince to rescue them, not even a "Saint Germain" to prevent the bills from mounting nor end the hundred-and-one ills to which flesh is heir.

Born at Newton, Kansas, on July 28, 1878, it was not until Ballard was fifty-two years of age that he assertedly met the Ascended Master Saint Germain on the side of a California mountain. And likewise, it was not until his good wife Edna was at the middle age of life that Aladdin rubbed his Wonderful Lamp and produced for her the money and power which, like most others, she had long been seeking.

Showing the struggles and ambitions of their early life, we now quote excerpts from letters written by people who knew one or both of the Ballards intimately:

"I have known Guy Ballard for more than thirty years," writes one of his friends, who is amazed at Ballard's sudden ascension into power. "He came to our home when I was a little girl, and at that time tried to be a medium. Edna, his wife, always has been ambitious, great for personal adornment, and has always been the man of the family."

"We have known Mr. and Mrs. Ballard for years," writes another party. "Mr. Ballard was a spiritualist in *medium*

Chicago, and practiced spiritualistic mediumship. Your diagnosis of them is practically correct."

"I have known Mr. Ballard for over thirty years," says still another. "He has been a medium during all these years. He told me he had made a great discovery and that he has the answer to all the difficulties we encounter."

We quote now from a much longer letter, written in the summer of 1938, which will give, perhaps, as vivid a picture of the Ballard background as it is possible to give:

"I know whereof I speak, for I have known the Ballards intimately for about twenty-six years. It was about 1915 we will say that I wrote a book on ancient Egypt. It had considerable to say about Egyptian Black Magic, and it was printed in an occult magazine. The story aroused considerable interest in several people . . . men who walk around apparently sane, but have a break somewhere in the brain fibre. Well these people wrote to me and many of them were most interesting correspondents. One of them later spent about four years in a mad house; still, he now walks around and proves himself to be a very subtle and dangerous person . . .

"I wrote to the Ballards for four years steady every week, then my husband died . . . They invited me to visit them in Chicago, which I did March 12, 1919. I lived with them for seven months, sharing their poverty, their sorrows, and their woes, for they were as poor as the proverbial church mouse . . .

"They induced me to finance the trip to California . . . The baby Eudonia [Donald] was just five years old . . . While in San Francisco this great idea of Guy's was born. We went to a fake ——— church, and there was a lot of chicanery. The Priest and Priestess sitting in two gold chairs with the twelve vestal virgins as the choir. Behind them was a great illuminated cross with flashing lights. During the service the very lightly clad virgins threw flowers among the audience. It was a scream. Afterwards came the Love Feast. A virgin held a basket of strips of bread and the audience were asked to join this holy order, which was non-sectarian. Another virgin held a loving cup of wine. Talk of hypnosis, would you believe it, over one hundred and fifty people went forward and partook of that sacrilegious feast, a parody upon the Lord's Supper!

"During this scene Guy's face was a study. He was enchanted with the show, but did not join the church. As soon as he reached the sidewalk, he could not stop talking about it . . . and from what I now hear, he has fashioned his church upon the same lines with his illuminated background. He could not stop talking about this laughable service . . .

"Guy Ballard had one obsession. He wanted to find a gold mine. He had dabbled a bit in mining prospecting, etc. He also studied hypnotism at this time, but was a bit afraid of it. His idea in bringing me to Chicago was that I might lead him to a gold mine, because I was a medium and had a spirit guide.

"My guide offended them both, for one night he told Edna that she had better stop right where they were, that she would become . . . [Here this woman quotes what the spirit guide said about Edna launching a great deception.]

"Thenceforth Edna had nothing more to do with my Ascended Master, but Guy thought he could manage him.

"So we traveled to the top of the Sierras, and lived in a tiny cottage next door to a gold mine. Every day either he and I walked out on the mountains, or Edna and he wandered to far distant places while I took care of the dream child. Guy was determined to find that gold mine. There was no money in the house and we lived upon practically nothing.

"One day in September, I remember it was the 21st, I was exploring the little village of about twenty houses, when I came across a tall white shaft numbered 10 up to 150.

" 'Why, what's that?' I asked, 'the game they play in Coney Island?'

" 'No, ma'm,' replied the native, 'that be the snow gauge. After this month you won't see anything but the roofs of the houses; even the horses go on snow shoes.'

"Well sir, I prayed hard to get out of discovering a gold mine. And strange to relate in a day or two a registered letter came to me inviting me to Ontario, Canada.

"I took the next train out of the nearest station, and that's the last I saw of the Ballards, until I ran into a group of people who with bated breath and fear in their eyes told me of the wonders they perform . . .

"I don't believe a word of the Mt. Shasta story. Poppycock! He got that idea wandering around the top of the Sierras. They would be gone for days together and camp out under the stars.

"The people I met in New York nearly mobbed me when I told them that the Ballards were frauds. One of them, not yet touched by their crazy ideas, gave me your letters, and this story of the killing of dear little trusting animals has induced me to write to you . . .

"I am told that thousands seem to be paralyzed or under a spell while they hold their meetings. He must have turned into a wizard of some sort. No wonder they bothered my life to try and give them the names of certain books . . .

"They are just very ordinary people, but clever. But again, they may be dealing in black magic. Guy was crazy about it."

From this graphic description of the Ballards' early history, two facts stand out in bold relief:

First, Guy Ballard and his wife Edna had what amounted to almost an obsession about gold mines. Second, they craved occult powers and mastery over others. Their books and platform utterances are clear evidence of these two cravings, and confirm what is said in this letter by a woman who had not, when she wrote it, read any of the Ballard books and had only attended one or two of their meetings.

Both were interested in, and no doubt had studied, hypnotism. When they first came to Los Angeles in 1935 Guy Ballard at every class would suddenly get up from his seat and start to make mesmeric passes over his audience. This would continue for many minutes, or until the audience would be in a suitably passive condition, enabling "Saint Germain" and his band of darkened "Spirits" to work on those susceptible to this kind of thing.

These mesmeric passes later were discontinued, no doubt for the reason it was all too apparent what these people were trying to do to their audiences. Perhaps, too, after such a good start in psychologizing their people there was no further need for being so objective in their hypnotic methods.

All through their books this same love of magical powers and mastery over others is shown. Saint Germain demolishes huge temples by the use of "Light Rays." Ballard and son Donald ape the great "Master" in the use of destructive forces.

When Mrs. Ballard was allegedly "Lotus, the Vestal Virgin," she was saved by the present Donald from being carried away by the slave of a "visiting prince" who wanted "to seize the vestal virgin for his bride." (p. 25, U. M.) We quote:

"The High Priest . . . [Donald in a past life] . . . raised his right hand and pointed directly at the slave. A flash of Flame shot forth like lightning, and the slave fell lifeless to the floor."

The visiting prince, all too careless of such death-dealing power, in a "blind rage" and "giving full vent to lust, rushed forward."

But again the priest raised his hand.

"The Flame flashed out a second time—and the prince

followed the fate of his former slave."

In this same book the senior Ballard also tells of his own deftness in the use of destructive forces; but instead of saving a fair vestal virgin in a past life, he in his present life saves a poor, lone widow from having her rich gold mine taken away from her by a wicked mine superintendent. We quote:

"He [the superintendent] lifted his steel cane and as I [Ballard] raised my hand to seize it—a White Flame suddenly shot forth flashing full in his face. He dropped to the floor as if struck by lightning." (p. 221, U. M.)

After this happy combination of both "magic power" and a rich "gold mine," Ballard proceeds in his next book to even tell about meeting face to face the *"God of Gold"*!

This great Being appeared to him, he says, while he was at the Rayborn mine in Colorado in 1932, and very unselfishly showed to him the location of a marvelous gold mine. And then the generous "Saint Germain"—still, however, holding on to his *"Spanish gold lost at sea"*—tells him: "After your return from the Far East, it will be opened up and one day the ore will be used for a special purpose . . ." (p. 280-281, M. P.)

But, alas! Ballard never achieved his dream of gold, except in his writings, and his magical powers only blossomed in his story books.

The Ballards wandered around on mountain tops with mediums and guides looking for the elusive metal, ever seeking, but never finding. And in their seeking after occult powers, they wandered from teacher to teacher. Not "Ascended Masters," mind you, as their books would have the credulous believe, but merely physical-plane mediums, occult lecturers, Hindus, Egyptians, and others in the magic world of metaphysics.

They became wandering metaphysical tramps, sat at the feet of earth-plane teachers too numerous to mention, and varied the business by getting through a few spiritualistic messages for themselves, as any other ordinary medium might.

They imbibed a little of Christian Science, read a bit of the Walter Method C.S., branched over to the Unity School at Kansas City, linked up with the Ancient and Mystical Order Rosae Crucis (A.M.O.R.C.), joined the Order of Christian Mystics, studied under Pelley the Silver Shirter, sat at the feet of some of the Swamis, read a little of Theosophy, looked into the magic of Yogi Philosophy and Oriental Mysticism, interested themselves in Baird T. Spalding and his "Masters of the Far East," which association gave them the idea, no doubt, of making all these metaphysical contacts produce the gold which their gold mines had failed to do—and which "Saint Germain," in a private dictation, said would *bring in more money than a gold mine!*

From this curious mixture of heterodoxy came forth the Ballard books—books which "Saint Germain" himself has said "none in the world had ever been written like them," which we can well believe.

They used what they wanted, changed and distorted what they desired, flavored the whole heterogeneous mixture with literary spice from novels of the Deadwood Dick type, salted it with pseudo-scientific facts from the pulp magazines, sugared it with a certain amount of goodness to catch the spiritual-hungry souls of this world, put it out in cellophane wrapping with an Arabian Nights' sparkle, labeled it the "Ascended Master Instruction of the Mighty I AM," privately imported by the three and only divinely-appointed Messengers, and sold it hot over the counters for large profit in the sacred Temples of the I AM.

And this is the strange and fantastic concoction that so many thousands of sincere people are being fed morning, noon, and night, and most of them will need a good psychological purging to get it out of their system.

CHAPTER 18

THE BALLARD GOLD MINE DEALS

As the antecedent history of the Ballards has been largely one of their seeking for magical powers and gold mines, it is no wonder that, living in need as they were, they should try to sell these things to their friends and to the public.

In October of 1938, as an aftermath of some old gold-mine deals, Guy Ballard was sued in Chicago by a woman who had years before looked upon him as a "Master," and a high spiritual teacher. The Chicago papers were full of it, devoting front-page headlines to the suit and to his gold-mine stock-selling projects of a previous decade.

The writer has no desire to reveal the mistakes of a man's life just for the mere sake of showing up those mistakes. God knows we all make enough of them. But here is a man who has made unprecedented claims for himself. He has publicly proclaimed the great purity of his life which caused him to be selected as the "Accredited Messenger" of Jesus (!) and the other members of the Cosmic Host. He has sold his public on these claims. They have bought his books and merchandise and have accepted his teachings completely on the strength of the sincerity, honesty, and truth of his claims.

It is conceivable that a man previous to a certain spiritual revelation might have lived a very unprincipled life, and then to have changed over completely. It would be manifestly unfair for some one to rake over those mistakes and publicly reveal them for the mere purpose of disconcerting this individual or turning people against him when he was so sincerely trying to "live the life."

The writer, for this reason, has sought mainly to analyze the Ballard books and public utterances, feeling that that alone should be sufficient to reveal the fraud and deception. But many people are not analytically minded, and must have evidence of some personal nature before they can recognize deception.

Besides, the Ballard movement has made history, and is no longer a private, secret affair. It is part of a great psychological wave of "escape mechanisms," or "salvation straws," both economic and religious, which people have been and are still holding on to, to save themselves from the tragic course of human events which now seems to engulf a good part of the world.

Therefore, as this is a history and study of the Ballard cult, it must deal with all phases of it, and certainly there can hardly be eliminated from it those gold-mine activities which have entered so dominantly into the affairs of this cult. When Ballard boldly comes out and makes statements concerning the saintliness of all his life in a last endeavor to keep his people buying his merchandise, then it seems necessary to show the real facts regarding his earlier life as well as more recent events and save additional people, if possible, from being deluded further.

What can one think of two people, whose history is known, who over their own signed names will make such a statement as follows?

"Mr. G. W. Ballard has never done a dishonest nor dishonorable thing in his entire life and never shall. We have never asked any human being for a thing, not even a dime nor a student list." (p. 19, Nov., 1938, v.)

In 1932 their Saint Germain assertedly said: "This beloved Sister and Brother have gone through thirty years of strenuous, conscious preparation for this work." (p. 244, D.)

It would appear from this statement that Ballard and

his wife have consciously been under the direction of great Teachers since 1902, but we ask whether the factual record of Guy Ballard's earlier life, as already revealed and to be additionally shown, would indicate any real direction from such great Teachers?

As further evidence that it does not, we quote from a reliable source as follows:

" . . . His activities were first in selling stock in an oil well in one of the southern states . . . He had a dream that it was going to 'gush' in February and sold more stock, but many Februaries have passed since then, and no gush.   His victims were mostly women.

"Seeing how gullible they were over buying imaginary things, he then sold almost the same list on another well, so they could get the money lost in the previous investment.

"Then Mr. Ballard joined with some others and cooked up the 'GOLD LAKE' in California, and practically the same list bit again . . ."

Now, this "Gold Lake" project in California, which our correspondent mentions above, gives a most revealing picture of the background of Ballardism.

On March 25, 1929—about a year and a half before Ballard said he met Saint Germain on the side of Mt. Shasta—Guy Ballard was indicted in Chicago by the Cook County Grand Jury on charge of "OBTAINING MONEY AND GOODS BY MEANS OF THE CONFIDENCE GAME." We have a copy of this indictment before us, and that is exactly the way it reads, capitals and all.

There were two such indictments, made on the sworn testimony of two women who had invested thousands of dollars in this "Lake of Gold" in California.   Warrants were issued for Ballard's arrest, but he was not apprehended, and did not stand trial.

Guy Ballard, during this time, was in Los Angeles using the assumed name of *Dick Gilbert*. It was in this city while on this enforced absence from Chicago that he gathered some of his material for *Unveiled Mysteries,* which was later supplemented by Mrs. Ballard's literary talents when he eventually was able to get back to Chicago.

He was absent for two years or more from his home town, during which time his book avers he was "traveling in the Far East." As a matter of fact, he was in the far *west*, on the Pacific Coast, traveling around attending metaphysical lectures and still looking for gold mines. There are a number of people in Los Angeles who knew him at that time, and he was certainly *not* in India.

Referring more specifically now to this "Lake of Gold" in California, which caused so many Chicagoans to lose their money, we quote from an unsolicited letter written by a woman who had invested in it:

Chcago, Ill.
Dec. 14, 1937

A friend, Mrs. ———, showed me your letter to her of recent date, and as I am one of the Ballards' victims, I am very glad to tell you a few things of how I have been treated . . .

I have known the Ballards for years, first meeting him through a mining proposition called the Gold Lake, and like everybody else I was fooled in the man.

I borrowed $200.00 from a friend to put in the Gold Lake, having already several hundred in it, and he begged me to loan him that $200 for his personal use he was so up against it and he said he would give me double the shares in the mine out of his holdings, etc.

It took me a long time to let him have it, and I asked him especially if he would be sure and give me credit on the books anyway so I would be sure to get my shares, and he promised, and which he NEVER did . . .

I have letters in which he says he does not owe me by 'Divine right.' . . .

A dear old lady in her 80's then, and has now passed away, felt so certain of this proposition going over she gave her all, her last $100 Ballard went and took from her . . .

He went to see a couple of elderly ladies, two sisters, one totally blind, and he got some money from them presumably for the Gold Lake, and he gave a receipt but never put it on the books.

(Signed) Miss————

This woman has many times tried to get Ballard to pay back the money he borrowed from her. In reply to one of her early letters to him in regard to this loan, he wrote her a letter which was postmarked Los Angeles.

Excerpts from this letter, which was written in Ballard's own handwriting, follow:

March 28, 1929

My dear Miss ————

God bless you, most kind friend. Your letter reached [me] after being forwarded twice, as I am changing about all the time trying to get something accomplished. The mining deals I came out here on did not work out . . .

I have been trying to secure employment west, but so far have not been able to get work . . . You do not seem to understand (from your letter) dear friend the terrible sacrifice I made to try to serve those people in that lake enterprise . . .

But some day God will place in my hands money to pay back every dollar that anybody ever assisted me with. At this time I haven't a dollar to help any body . . .

When God sees fit to help me to success, I will be so happy and grateful to return every dollar of kindness that has been extended to me. Until then I am powerless to help.

. . . I know so well everyone who condemns me will be consumed by their own hatred.

I am leaving for Nevada at once. If anything comes into my hands to help, I will gladly do it. A friend is trying to help me get on my feet again.

(Signed) Guy W. Ballard

This hand-written letter of Mr. Ballard's gives a very good picture of his life and wanderings just prior to his alleged contact with "Saint Germain" on the side of Mt. Shasta.

Does that life, with all of its admitted inability to cope with circumstances, seem to be good material for a great "Master" to work with?

Why should this man, who admittedly was duped in a mining deal, be selected out of one hundred and thirty million people to "Save America" from all its economic and spiritual ills?

Why should this particular "Messenger," of whom, assertedly, Jesus himself says has *"not made one single mistake from the beginning,"* a man who "for thirty years has been consciously preparing for this work," have been selected when there were records against him of having made mistakes?

But let us see the sequel of this correspondence.

This woman who was duped, hearing Ballard was back in Chicago selling people on his "Mighty I AM," and thinking that the "I AM" would surely give him enough money to pay the small debt he had so faithfully promised to pay, wrote him again.

His reply follows:

February 11, 1934

Miss ———

Your letter received after some delay. I have no money for myself, you or anyone else.

If you will remind yourself of the thought and feeling of condemnation, hatred and the wish to take away the liberty of God's children, then you will understand why you have no position, money or health. For what you think, feel and desire for another you draw with invincible power into your own life and experience whether you believe it or not . . .

When you joined others with the intent to take away my freedom, you deprived yourself of every divine right of any assistance from me.

However, at some future time should abundance come into my hands I would gladly help you if only to return good for evil. May God's Love and Light ever enfold you.

(Signed) Guy W. Ballard

Not to be put off by any such letter, this woman again

wrote Ballard pointing out that his accusations in the second paragraph were totally untrue, but that IF they were, the same thing would apply in his case also and be the reason why he, too, had "no money for himself, his creditors, or anyone else."

Then referring to the third paragraph in which Ballard had said, "You deprived yourself of every divine right of any *assistance* from me," she said: "Let me make this clear to you. By DIVINE right you owe me the $200 which you borrowed in cold cash for your 'personal use.' I am not asking you for any 'help,' 'assistance,' or CHARITY . . . I am asking only for what is mine . . . If you have not got the $200 to send at one time, then pay by the week."

And what was the "Accredited Messenger's" reply to this righteous request?   It is given below:

Miss ———
    Your second letter received. I have informed you this outer form has no money to assist you and no income to promise you or anyone anything definite.
    In spite of reports to you, we do not own a home and no money is being received for the instruction that is being given. In regard to the letter that you sent me, I simply say God Bless you.

                            (Signed) Guy W. Ballard

Remember at this time (1934) Ballard, for nearly four years had been under the special training of "Saint Germain," at least so he said, having met that gentleman on the side of Mt. Shasta in 1930, and at that time this great "Master" for his amusement had plucked a ten dollar gold piece from the mountain air with all the ease of a frock-coated magician.

He had also shown Ballard an entire room filled with coins and nuggets, and "Spanish gold lost at sea"—and had presented him with a gold mine or two.

Yet, despite the magic of this great "Master" and the

wealth of "Spanish gold" and Colorado gold mines, this man could not pay this poor, deaf, struggling woman the $200.00 he had borrowed from her—not even a few dollars a week!

And this money has not been paid to this day, despite the fact that these people and their "staff" tour the country in princely style and live off the fat of the land.

How different is their front to the world! How can they write and speak the consummate nonsense of their saintliness and goodness that they do?

"Dear ones," said Ballard through his own vocal cords to his San Francisco audience on January 23, 1938, "the Messengers should be a mighty example to you. They have never asked for a dime in their lives." (pp. 391-392, A. M. L.)

And yet in the city of Chicago and elsewhere there are a number of people from whom Ballard has begged and borrowed money. Despite this, he and his wife had the audacity to publish over their own signatures the following moral instruction to their people—as though they had lived up to it one hundred per cent themselves!

"Beloved Young America! . . . If you borrow either money or things, FEEL your responsibility and see that you return them to the one who was kind enough to accommodate you. Just because someone is kind and willing to make things easier for you is no reason you should fail to remember that the thing loaned to you should be returned . . . Lovingly, MR. AND MRS. G. W. BALLARD." (pp. 33-34, Feb., 1938, v.)

Ask the scores of people who either lent money to Ballard or his wife, or invested it in the "Lake of Gold," whether these "Accredited Messengers of the Ascended Masters" have lived up to precepts they so glibly give others.

CHAPTER 19

TRIUMPHANT ENTRY INTO CHICAGO

In an earlier chapter it was described how during the first part of October, 1934, the then little-known Ballards jumped the train out of Chicago and started on their conquest to save heathen America.

For some reason—which most of their students did not understand—it was not until exactly *four years later* (October, 1938) that they publicly returned to Chicago to hold classes.

Not that the heathen in that particular city in those four years did not need the saving grace of the "Mighty I AM," but, as we shall find, they did not lecture there because of certain other and quite valid reasons.

In those four years the "Accredited Messengers of Saint Germain" had achieved astonishing success. They had lectured practically in every large city throughout the United States, and in certain favorite "I AM" watering places they had returned many times. But back to their own home town of Chicago they simply wouldn't go to hold public classes.

"What was the trouble?" "Why had Chicago failed?" "Was a prophet really without honor in his own city as Jesus had said?" All these and many other questions filtered through the minds of the good Chicago students. "Was Chicago as wicked as that?" they asked.

A couple of years previously the Ballards had made an abortive effort to lecture in Chicago. Saint Germain had come through with these instructions to their Assistant Director: "Take a class of four days in Chicago on your way east . . . Four days will fulfill all that is necessary."

But before the Assistant Director could make the necessary arrangements even for that short length of time, all was changed. The Ballards had evidently received disquieting news from the "windy city," and the Saint Germain order was countermanded.

The following excerpt from a letter received by the writer from a former close associate will no doubt explain why even the great Saint Germain's order was not obeyed:

"In our days of innocence we heard of a concerted effort to have him [Ballard] arrested in public if he ever came to Chicago in a class, and we went to St. Louis to warn them. And this is what they said:

" '*WE ARE NOT COMING BACK TO CHICAGO UNTIL OUR DEBTS ARE OUTLAWED.*'

"Then they entered into a personal argument as to how long that would be, and he said: 'That will be in about *two years.*' She said: 'No, I think it will be in about eighteen months.' "

This episode occurred in October, 1936. The Ballards returned to Chicago in October, 1938—just *two years* after Ballard had made the above statement that he would *not return until his debts were outlawed;* which he thought would be in about two years.

And so the Ballards, after an unexplained absence of four years, did return publicly to their own city. But even then, it seems that this return was more or less forced upon them. Their critics on one hand were saying that they were afraid to go back to their own home town because of their past, and on the other hand the Chicago faithful were beseeching them to come. So after personally making reasonably sure it was safe, they handed over their fears to Saint Germain and the Ascended Host—and went.

Some time and care had evidently been taken to prepare the ground for a triumphant entry. Their publicity agents were very much on the job, and the Ether-waves were hot with the news of the arrival of the "Accredited Messengers of Saint Germain." Newspapers published their pictures in full "I AM" regalia on front pages. Large headlines announced their lecture topics from day to day.

"*Fount of Youth Claimed*," was one of the headings. "*5000 Hear New 'I AM' Evangelism*," said another. "*Thousands Bask in 'Great Light' at Cult Meeting*," said still another, and so on.

Altogether, it was a most fitting reception to two Chicagoans who had gone out into the world and made good, and had now returned to the city of their first love to have laurels heaped upon them. A good prophet was surely *not* without honor in his own city!

It was too cold in the windy city for palm leaves—Los Angeles would have been a more fitting place—but Chicago had to have her day. She gave the Ballards a royal welcome, even though instead of the Messengers riding into the city in the traditionally humble style, as becomes high spiritual teachers of Oriental countries, they used flashy motor cars—three "*golden colored*" ones for the two senior Ballards and staff, and an "*electric blue*" for son Donald.

Quoting from a special article from the *Chicago Daily News* on the great event, dated October 12, 1938, we learn that the "high priest and priestess" of the movement "are packing the big opera house with throngs of well-dressed, intelligent-looking following and recent converts," and that it is estimated "when the 10-day Chicago sojourn of the Ballards comes to a colorful finish, 50,000 persons will have heard the story of the 'ascending Masters, and 'vibrations,' and that thousands of dollars will have been deposited in the little yellow envelopes."

"Have you a lot of bills?" Mrs. Ballard at one point asked her audience, according to an article in the *Chicago Herald & Examiner* of October 8, 1938. "The great light wants you to pay them, but every irritation in your emotional body prevents it. Receive the light and the bills will be paid."

What kind of "emotional irritation" was preventing Ballard from paying his own bills, or paying the little woman who had lent him $200.00 in good faith?

"The Ballards made no secret of the fact that their cup of material happiness is full to overflowing," says an article in the *Chicago Herald & Examiner* of October 10, 1938.

"You, too, can enjoy the same benefits, they say, if you follow their teachings . . . 'But it was not always thus,' said blond Mrs. Ballard: 'We didn't know where our next meal was coming from when we started our work.' "

With all this publicity about paying bills and demonstrating meals, the generous and popular Ballards, as was to be expected, became more popular than ever. For who doesn't want to pay old bills and eat a good meal?

Success at last in this city had crowned their efforts. The large and beautiful opera house was packed with an expectant and applauding audience. The stage was banked with ferns and flowers, and the Ballards themselves, dressed in their very best, looked very affluent and even majestic. Over a radio set-up on the stage, their words were broadcast to listening thousands who could not get to the big opera house.

"These utterances," says the *Chicago Daily News*, "fascinate his terraced ranks of followers—they hang upon the cryptic pronouncements . . . "

"Men women, and children from every walk of life sat enthralled," says another news writer.

"A myriad eyes fastened rapturously upon the brilliantly decorated stage," commented still another.

Chicago had accepted them . . . her children had returned . . . all had apparently been forgiven.

But neither the happy Messengers nor their glorified Masters—who know everything—were aware that cruel fate was soon to take a hand. That despite all this show and glamour, the Chicago past of the Accredited Messengers was still grinding. That soon there was to be an event which would shake the confidence of thousands in these glorious people.

"Kick out deceit and treachery from your lives," implored Mr. Ballard, according to the article in the *Daily News*. "I know when any deceit or harmful activity comes into this class room. If I don't, Saint Germain does."

And Mrs. Ballard, in her gorgeous raiment, waxed just as eloquent.

"I have touched Saint Germain, just as I touch you now," said she, according to the *Herald & Examiner* article. "His flesh is something like ours, but it is alabaster white, and a light flows from it . . . The blood of Ascended Beings turn to gold when they leave the mortal sphere."

The *Daily News* article describes her as " . . . a queenly personage in a silk gown of geranium hue, with broad ribbon trailers suspended from the shoulders in lieu of an opera train. Her hair is arranged in a coronet of white curls . . . she sits placidly in a gold-and-ivory chair."

Thus did Chicago accept her very own. *"How those decrees do work!"* must have thought the Ballards as they read these publicity articles or from the decorated stage surveyed this magnificent victory over their hectic past in this city.

"They say we dared not come to Chicago," Mrs. Ballard is reported to have said, "but we are here!" And then with a dramatic gesture, she added: *"So what?"*

This "So what" part of the history of the Ballard movement will have to be included under a different heading than that of their triumphant entry into Chicago. The "Accredited Messengers of Saint Germain" might have made a triumphant entry, as these news items would indicate, but they were fated soon to make a different kind of exit!

CHAPTER 20

THE BALLARD PAST BOBS UP AGAIN

Into this Chicago "I AM" heaven, which the Ballards had so carefully prepared for themselves, entered the wicked serpent.

It did not tell the woman, as in the traditional story, but it seems that it did tell the Chicago authorities to taste and investigate the particular brand of apple sauce the Ballards were selling the good Chicago people.

It appears that the bailiff's office particularly tasted of this apple concoction, and apparently thought it was too good to keep to themselves. So one evening, shortly after Mrs. Ballard's "So what?" query, a duly appointed bailiff invaded the peace of the Chicago "I AM" heaven and publicly served Ballard with a summons to appear in court to answer certain charges.

The following morning the Chicago dailies ran big front page headlines about the suit.

The *Chicago Herald & Examiner*, on the morning of October 14, 1938, came out with a big two-inch headline, reading:

"WOMAN SUES 'GREAT I AM.'"

Below was a large photograph of Ballard being served the summons, and there was nothing else on the front page with the exception of a description of this "I AM" suit. The photograph shows Ballard sitting at a desk in the lobby occupied with his favorite pastime of autographing books (freshly sold at $2.50 to $3.00 per copy), while his startled followers stand and gesticulate wildly around him in their efforts to prevent the bailiff from carrying out his duty of serving the papers.

Underneath the photograph it states that the "Accredited Messenger" was "served the summons despite pandemonium among the followers."

Then on page three was the story, from which we quote in part:

"In a stormy scene in the lobby of the Civic Opera House, Guy W. Ballard, 'Accredited Messenger' of the 'Great I AM Presence,' was served with a summons in a $10,906.55 suit last night.

"Ballard was surrounded by a dozen or more of his followers in the Civic Opera lobby when C——, chief bailiff of the civil branch of the sheriff's office, attempted to serve the summons.

"Men and women shouted, tried to push the bailiff from the lobby. Others seized Ballard's arm, and sought to draw him away. In a loud voice, C—— read the summons."

Picture the scene. Here was a man who had publicly stated:

"My earthly pilgrimage is finished . . . I am here in this atomic structure on extended time . . . nothing this human form can do can be recorded upon my life stream."

And yet, here he was, in his own "I AM" heaven, having his own record read and recorded, and there was nothing he could do about it. Nor could his followers who crowded around him wildly decreeing and gesticulating.

The record follows. in part, according to this bill which was filed in the Superior Court:

"Some time prior to and about the years 1923 or 1924 the plaintiff became acquainted with the defendant, Guy W. Ballard, who represented himself to be interested in and learned in said mysticism and occult arts and sciences.

"Through the mutual interest of said plaintiff and of said defendant, the said defendant obtained the confidence and trust of the plaintiff, and the defendant, abusing and taking advantage of said confidence and trust imposed by the plaintiff in the defendant, requested from the plaintiff and obtained from her advances of large sums of money . . . under various pretexts and reasons, such as personal loans for current expenses . . . etc., etc."

Virtually all the Chicago newspapers that morning ran headlines and stories about this suit against the "*Mighty I AM*"—the name they dubbed Ballard.

The *Chicago Tribune* headed their story: "The Great I AM Runs Afoul of a Cynical Mystic." The *Chicago Daily News* captioned their article: "Mundane Bailiff Invades Mystic Realm to Get Man." The *Chicago Daily Times* styled theirs: " 'Great I AM' Face to Face with Cash Suit." The *Chicago American* said: "Woman Sues 'I AM' Leader for $10,000."

We quote in part from the *Chicago American* article:

"Miss ——, a little, grayhaired woman of about 60, is employed as a housekeeper . . . Her life savings, gleaned from her work as a servant for some of Chicago's best known society families, were given to Ballard, she said today, to invest in what he called 'The Cottonwood Trust' to exploit 'The Lake of Gold' in California, supposedly a mining project.

"Loss of the $6,775 which Miss —— says she entrusted to the 'Mighty I AM' before he left town, made her unable to bring criminal proceedings at that time. She visited the state's attorney's office, Miss —— explained, but was told she would be required to post some money if a policeman were to be sent after the 'Mighty I AM.' She explained:

" '*But he had taken all my money and I didn't have any left to put up to have him arrested.*'

"The Ballards, she said, were well-known along the North Shore as far as Milwaukee, but more in servants' quarters than in drawing rooms. She explained: '*He had a very large following of North Shore servants when he was operating as 'The Master.'* A lot of servants followed him.' "

Asked by one of the newspaper reporters if she had attended any of the Civic Opera House meeting, she retorted:

"I should say not! I was afraid I would lose my temper and would expose him right there!"

One of the Ballard decrees reads:

"Compel all that consciously opposes This Work in any way to annihilate itself and blast its own cause and effect from existence forever!"

Another one reads:

"Prevent the press, reporters, and all outer channels from making any false statements about this work . . . SILENCE everything of that kind throughout the world forever!"

Nevertheless, despite the alleged power of these decrees, the reporters and the press would not be silenced. The next morning there followed further revelations about Ballard's "Lake of Gold."

We quote from the *Chicago Herald & Examiner* of October 15 in an article headed, "SOUGHT IN GOLD SWINDLE; CULT LEADER BEGS FAITH":

" . . . Many other persons were known to have invested money. Blue sky authorities said these investors lost $200,000, some estimates going as high as $500,000. An investigator sent to look at the California property of the company reported title to the land was doubtful and that not more than $5,000 had ever been spent there. There was a rough board building, he said, but no evidence of mining machinery."

This article further stated:

"All that was needed, investigators say they were told, was to drain the lake and take out the precious metals with scoop shovels."

This "Gold Lake" project in California which Guy

Ballard and his associates sold to credulous people was a happening of a dozen years or more ago, and was preceded, as we have seen, by his gold-seeking adventures upon mountain tops. But all this was really only the beginning of Ballard's sensational gold-mine career—a mere preliminary skirmish, as it were, before the real campaign.

Since then he has really become proficient in manufacturing gold mines, and he makes them bigger and better all the time. When once one puts his hand to the plow, or rather his mind to the great task of manufacturing gold mines on a mass production basis, there is no turning back. He has to make new, bigger, and better gold mines, or else the shortcomings of the old ones will be too apparent to those who signed on the dotted line.

It is not surprising, therefore, to find that a few years later the lone California "Gold Lake" blossomed into three marvelous Colorado "Gold Mines." And in Ballard's book the great Saint Germain tells about them.

"This body of ore," said the great Master, referring to the second one of the mines, "contains over twenty million dollars in gold, clear and above all operating expenses." (p. 40, M. P.)

And as if this were not enough gold to forever satisfy or even satiate a gold-loving appetite, Saint Germain's magic eye leads him to another great discovery.

"I wish to say," says this gold-finding Master, "there is another great ore-body not half a mile from the 'Master Discovery,' as you call it, which I will reveal during your next trip to the mine, three days hence. As the claims are all patented and the deeds in your hands, they will be safe, until your return from the East in two years." (p. 273, M. P.)

But unfortunately for Saint Germain's "patented" gold claim and Ballard's "deeds" placed in his hands, the unbelieving Commissioner of Mines of the State of Colorado is quite skeptical about the matter, as will be discovered in the following letter received from the Commissioner himself, dated March 15, 1937, at Denver:

"I know of no marvelous mine in Colorado owned by one Daniel Rayborn, and I know nothing of G. W. Ballard . . . We frequently hear of 'Mystic' mines in Colorado and other states, and people have spent years and years looking for them, but I have never heard of one that has been found. I look upon them as fakes; in fact, I know it is a fake pure and simple."

The three marvelous, though hypothetical, gold mines having served their particular purpose in luring buyers for their book (why else should they be there?), the Ballards turned their attention to manufacturing out of whole cloth a *new* sort of gold mine. Not even the genie in *Aladdin and His Wonderful Lamp* could have ever thought of it.

This is the way of it. For years the Ballards have been telling their audiences about the dangerous "Gas Belts" which are supposed to lie under some of our most populous cities and which, they say, are the cause of earthquakes. Many of the susceptible ones in these cities became extremely jittery over the "Gas Belts" under their feet and joined the cult to protect themselves—for *only* the Ballard "decrees" could save these cities from utter destruction.

That of course was very much in line with this cult's usual procedure in psychologizing their people through fear, but in this case they went a step further and combined another mainspring of human action.

It was to Mrs. G. W. Ballard, co-originator and prime mover of the cult, that the idea first came. In her efforts to "Save America" from these earthquakes—which they said were "long past due"—she conceived the brilliant idea of changing all these restless "Gas Belts" into "*pure metallic gold*"!

That was a stroke of genius which naturally did not go unrewarded, for who wouldn't want to join a movement which would guarantee to change ordinary sewer gas, or its deeper-lying relative, into pure metallic gold?

To get "saved" and "rich" at one time is motive enough for anybody. So a gas-converting decree was drawn up by the decree-maker of the establishment, Mrs. G. W. Ballard, and the blessed, gold-loving students shouted it from coast to coast in their heroic efforts to "Save America"—a nation which already has more gold stored away in the ground than it knows what to do with, some $20,000,000,000 worth!

To date, latest news from the decreeing front indicates that the I AM-ers have not been successful in accomplishing their great alchemical feat, for their high command, Mrs. G. W. Ballard, still speaks of the earthquake danger. The "gas" menace, therefore, is still with us, an ever-present worry in the I AM-ers' troubled world.

The luring of the Ballard hopeful by means of the bright yellow metal still continues, but always it is the *new* and not the old "gold mine" to which attention is called.

Guy Ballard, shortly after his old stock-selling activities in his "Lake of Gold" project bobbed up in Chicago, stated to his Los Angeles audience:

"In India there are five great mountain peaks," and referring to one of these peaks, he added: "There is gold enough in that one peak to a hundred times pay the debts of the world. I know this to be true." (p. 28, March, 1939, v.)

Despite all his assurance of debt-paying gold in India the Chicago papers wouldn't let Ballard's old "Lake of Gold" in California alone. He tried his best to switch the minds of people off to a gold-studded mountain peak in far-away India, but this fabulous "Gold Lake" which had suddenly reappeared out of his past was a bit more real to the scores of people who had lost their life-savings in it. It had to be explained in some way, and in the following chapter we will see how the Ballards made answer to it.

CHAPTER 21

HOW THE BALLARDS ANSWERED THE CHICAGO SUIT

The Chicago suit, with its revealing connection with Ballard's "Lake of Gold," was no doubt one of the embarrassing moments for the two dictators.

They had not expected it. They had had their agents working in Chicago trying to get the two indictments withdrawn. They had contacted the two signers in an effort to get them to withdraw the charges; and it appears they were successful in doing this, for the indictments were nolle prossed in July, 1938. It therefore seemed safe to return in October, at which time, owing to the Illinois statute of limitation, they seemed to be assured their old debts would be outlawed.

Months before, when they were in nearby Detroit the early part of May, 1938, they had been looking forward to their Chicago return. At that time hundreds of Chicago students had come down to Detroit to hear the Messengers, as these Messengers could not for very good reasons at that time go to them. Notice now what these Chicago students were told:

"I congratulate you beloved ones of Chicago," said the Goddess of Liberty (!), "in having the Power and Action of Light . . . which drew you here in this great number. (Applause) Be patient, beloved ones, the time is near at hand, when the *Power of Light will sweep Chicago!* (Applause) Mankind should understand the importance of letting the Wisdom of These Great Ones, Who have come forth, regulate and govern what the Messengers do and where they will go!" (p. 9, June, 1938, v., our italics.)

And so the Ballards and their "Power of Light" did "sweep Chicago" with much show of glitter in a grand and triumphant entry, but this unexpected suit shook the glitter out, and made it necessary for them to brazen through the crisis in some way. How they did it will now be shown.

On the following evening after the papers were served, and "pandemonium reigned among their followers," the Ballards attempted to make some sort of answer. We quote from the *Chicago Herald & Examiner* of October 15, article headed: "Sought in Gold Swindle; Cult Leader Begs Faith."

"People of America," called Mrs. Ballard, in a broadcast from the platform, "we ask you, regardless of anything you have heard or read, to believe that the work of the Mighty I AM Presence and the Ascended Masters is clean and honest and is the truth. Regardless of all untruth that has been spoken or printed, we never have asked for a dime and never tried to draw any human being from any other creed or belief. I say this to the whole earth: Mr. Ballard has never done a dishonest or dishonorable thing in his life and never shall!"

Mrs. Ballard then turned the microphone over to Ballard, who said:

"Thank you, beloved Lotus! It is incredible that any one should wish to be vicious to us, who have never asked one thing for ourselves. I have never claimed I was a Master, and any one who says I did is a liar!"

That certainly should settle the matter once and for all, but we might gently inject the thought that Guy Ballard has perhaps made more claims for himself than has any other person in America. Even Father Divine only permits his followers to *call* him "God." He doesn't come right out and proclaim it, having retained a little modesty in the matter. But Mr. Ballard comes right out in print and speech and has "God, the Mighty I AM" give a stirring sales talk all about Guy Ballard!

The following modest claims for himself are made:

He lives in a *"body of immortal endurance."* (page 390, M. P.) There *"isn't anything in the universe that he fears,"* and *"nothing can be recorded upon his life stream."* (August, 1935, Lecture.)

He is *"a free being and could leave at any moment."* (p. 11, Sept., 1938, v.) *"No one on earth can take his place."* (p. 13, Nov., 1938, v.)

He is *"as humble as humbleness can be."* (p. 6, Dec., 1938, v.) *"Has not made one single mistake from the beginning."* (p. 15, Feb., 1937, v.)

He *"can decree and it is fulfilled almost instantly."* (p. 77, A. M. D.) But for him and his good wife Edna *"mankind would have perished from the earth."* Jan. 7, 1938, G. L.)

And lastly, believe it or not, he *"has never asked for a dime in his life!"* (pp. 391-392, A. M. L.)

Surely, if Guy Ballard is all of the above, then he is not only a "Master" but something more!

Why call someone a prevaricator (to use a gentler term than he did) because this same somebody said he claimed to be a "Master" fifteen years ago? Does he not today claim to be something very much more than that?

Fortunately for the Accredited Messengers of Saint Germain, the Chicago suit against Guy Ballard and its past gold mine connections was not publicized very much in other cities. The Ballards did everything they could to keep their students from believing it was anything but a "vicious attack."

In the next issue of their official journal after the Chicago suit, the Ballards attempted to pour a little miracle-working oil over the troubled waters of the movement. They referred evasively to this Chicago suit, and cunningly headed their article: "Our Ascended Master Miracle"! We quote:

"We wish to express our deepest Eternal Love and Gratitude, and to thank every 'I AM' student for the Love, Loyalty, unflinching Courage, Self-control and Assistance with which all handled the intrusion of discord which attempted to touch the Chicago Class.

"Mr. G. W. Ballard has never done a dishonest nor dishonorable thing in his entire life and never shall. We have never asked any human being for a thing, not even a dime nor a student list; and all who know us even slightly know THAT IS THE TRUTH!

"We have given all and asked nothing in return . . .

"We all called in this Chicago Class for GIGANTIC ASCENDED MASTER MIRACLES . . . to come out of even the slightest attempt to discredit or interfere . . . THE RECENT OCCURRENCE HAS TURNED INTO JUST THAT . . . MR. AND MRS. G. W. BALLARD." (pp. 19-20, Nov., 1938, v.)

The Ballards, however, fail to explain just how it is that "pandemonium among their followers" could at the same time be "unflinching courage and self-control." Nor just how it was that "intrusion of discord" was turned into a "GIGANTIC ASCENDED MASTER MIRACLE."

The miracle, of course, lies in the fact that the students should accept such a statement. There was certainly no other miracle.

The crisis in Chicago was so great that the Ballards had to call out an entirely *new* "Ascended Master"—or rather in this case it was a "Lady Master," who they said was none other than the "GODDESS OF LIGHT"!

"She has opened the Door of the Ascended Masters' Octave to the earth," explained Ballard to the Chicago faithful, and added: "It is an unheard of thing in the history of the world . . . (applause)." (p. 5, Nov., 1938, v.)

"I want to say to you," said the Goddess upon being introduced, and conveniently using Ballard's vocal cords, "that if good were not to come out of the experience which occurred at your class recently, this Messenger could have stood and without a word released the Power of a Light Ray and *those individuals would still remain standing in their tracks;* but he would not do it." (p. 10, our italics.)

And there you are! What self-control it must have been for Ballard to have withheld the "lightning" that would have stopped the poor process server right in his tracks; which was something the excited efforts of his students failed to do.

We are glad that Ballard didn't forget himself and absent-mindedly let it loose. No wonder students run to the cover of the "Mighty I AM" protection and dare not say anything to incur the Ballard disfavor.

" . . . That same Power," continues the Goddess, "could have been released had it chosen to do so. There are no human persons nor creation that could stop it. . ." (p. 11.)

But fortunately for the process server, this terrific power was withheld. To be stopped by a bullet is one thing, but to be stopped by Mr. Ballard's little "Light Ray" would certainly make any self-respecting officer a trifle shamefaced.

The Goddess agreeably concurs with the Ballards that it was indeed a miracle:

"Out of this occurrence has really come an Ascended Master Miracle," she says. "You can all well rejoice that the Messenger was strong enough and calm enough to go serenely on and let it take place. It has been the means of dissolving and removing from your Chicago forever the resistance which has been here for many years." (p. 11.)

In the Ballard official Group Letter, or report to their students, under date of November 20, 1938, there are many references to the Chicago suit:

"On Thursday night a vicious attack was made on our Beloved Mr. Ballard while he was quietly autographing books in the foyer of the beautiful Chicago Civic Auditorium."

This *"vicious attack"* consisted of the process server presenting Ballard formally with a summons. Photographers also aimed their cameras at him while he was being served. No real casualties were reported, such as might be suggested by a vicious "attack."

"A few minutes later," continues the official report, "we heard newsboys crying out 'Extra—all about the I AM suit.' It was such a complete surprise that we purchased a copy, and then read to our amusement . . . "

Why should this occurrence have been "such a complete surprise" with the all-knowing Saint Germain around? And how much "amusement" did the newspaper article really give?

Evidently, Saint Germain was away on "European business" on this "miracle" night, for it was not until the following day that he arrived to do battle against such vicious individuals:

"Five of the most vicious black magicians in America were seized last night!" he told the applauding audience. Commenting on the reasons for the suit, he said:

"The woman who made this charge, some years ago, for no reason at all, became very angry at the Messengers."

The little matter of $6,775 is of course "no reason at all" to a wealthy "Ascended Master" with his hoard of "Spanish gold lost at sea" and three Colorado gold mines. But it *was* for the little woman who had slaved all her life to save it from her meager earnings.

"She KNOWS that the charge is NOT true!" continued Saint Germain. "She KNOWS very well that this Messenger did NOT receive her money, and I know it!

" . . . The vicious individuals who came into that lobby last night," said Saint Germain, "are dealing with Me, and not the Messenger! I always abide My time.

"I say to the newspapers who were unfortunate enough

to print that, they too must pay the penalty for it . . . Now begins the destruction of every one who allows such things to continue . . . I say to every newspaper in the land—take heed! I am always present and watching everything, and when I am ready I will act."

Surely, after this fair warning from the great Saint Germain himself, none of us would like to be newspaper people—certainly not *Chicago* ones. Such as they can only wait the dire and inevitable consequences of their own heedlessness. The suspense must be terrific.

While Saint Germain in this speech spent most of his allotted stage time threatening Chicago news reporters and editors, he still had time to praise his tried and tested "Accredited Messengers":

"Beloved Ones," said he to the Chicago audience, "when I chose him [Ballard] and the beloved Lotus to be the Messengers of My Work, I knew every thought and feeling that is in their Beings. There is not one impure nor dishonest thought in their whole Life! (tremendous applause) . . . This beloved Messenger rendered a service last night for which all America one day will bless him! (Again tremendous applause as the huge audience arose to their feet!)" (p. 2, Nov. 20, 1938, G. L.)

This, in brief, is how the Accredited Messengers of Saint Germain and the Ascended Masters answered the Chicago suit. But it appears that the "Gigantic Ascended Master Miracle," which assertedly happened at Chicago, didn't influence the Chicago authorities to nullify and make void the suit brought by the little woman who had invested her all in Ballard's "Lake of Gold." The "Miracle" didn't take care of that little point.

However, eleven days before the trial was to come up—on December 29, 1939—an event occurred which was to make it forever impossible for Guy Ballard, defendant, to satisfy the claimant in this suit. The details of this will be told in the last chapter.

CHAPTER 22

HOW "SAINT GERMAIN" KEPT WAR OUT OF EUROPE

It is now well, in this history of "Ascended Master Miracles" and other stirring events, that we tell the equally stirring story of how the "*War Entity of the World*" was consumed and war kept out of Europe.

This "War Entity," according to the Ballard literature, is none other than the "Beast" of Revelations. He is a sort of black magician par excellence, with a body of unusual proportions; that is, he *had* before the Ballards started to "work" on it.

The *head* of the monster, Saint Germain, said, "*was over New York*," and explained that it had "largely to do with communistic activity." (p. 17, Aug., 1938, v.)

However, he is rather vague as to the exact location of the other parts of the monster, but it appears that its "*body rests over Europe*." (p. 468, A. M. L.)

Many were the decrees of the students directed against this psychic monster. For years they had tried to dissolve it. It was only, however, during the Shrine class in Los Angeles in the summer of 1938 that their decrees seemed to have any effect.

During the Shrine class, Saint Germain came forth to make a momentous announcement.

"Beloved ones," he said, " . . . You know how long, these three and a half years, that your call has been made for the dissolving of the war entity. That has begun! (Wild applause)

"It began on the opening day of this Class, when the Great Cosmic Light was again released. It began with the head over New York, with the eye which sees the weakness of mankind. *That eye sees no more!* (Wild applause again)

"All around the body of the war entity of the world there is a Powerful Blue Flame which is steadily and surely moving in upon the form, its body of substance.

"It is Our hope that by the end of this Class, the war entity shall have been dissolved . . . It only means a continued pounding away on these Mighty Decrees . . .

"I firmly believe that the war will soon cease in Europe and the Orient. (Wild applause)." (p. 1, July 26, 1938, G. L.)

The above encouraging statement of Saint Germain's about the ceasing of the civil war in Spain and the war of aggression in China was made on July 2, 1938. Two days later, on the Fourth of July, after a lot of decreeing by the students, he came forth to report extraordinary progress in dissolving the monster.

"Beloved students," he said, "I bring you great encouragement: *more than half the war entity of Europe has been dissolved!* (Wild applause)" (p. 2, July 26, 1938, G. L.)

Saint Germain didn't say whether our little American yen for setting off firecrackers and other explosives on the Fourth had anything to do with dissolving half the "War Entity," or not, but we can well believe it.

Then on the last day of the Shrine Class, July 10, right on schedule, Saint Germain came forth fresh from the troubled diplomatic circles of Europe to make his report.

"Beloved students of the Light," he said, "We have the most glorious news of the centuries for you today. At 12:00 o'clock noon today, your time here, *THE LAST VESTIGE OF THE WAR ENTITY OF THE WORLD WAS CONSUMED!"*

"For a moment," continues this report, "the audience was spellbound; then as the Greatness of it broke upon us, the huge audience arose as one man, and unleashed one mighty wave of applause that continued on and on, so great was our heart's rejoicing. The war entity of the world, referred to in the Bible as the Beast, was consumed!" (p. 3.)

With this timely destruction of the "War Entity of the World" one would have thought that hostilities in Europe and Asia would cease forthwith. But not so! Europe on the contrary showed immediately an increased flare for war, culminating in that fatal crisis the latter part of September, 1938, the historic Chamberlain-Hitler peace conferences at Munich.

But nevertheless and notwithstanding, the Ballards even here took credit for saving Europe. Note the following ingenious statements:

"Our Great Cosmic Mother, the Mighty Goddess of Liberty, gave the closing night Dictation . . . The date was September 25, 1938, when the frightful situation in Europe could have burst forth into another world conflagration. The Ascended Masters had asked the I AM students to redouble their earnest call for their fellow man in Europe. We did.

"Telegrams flashed to all the large Groups of students everywhere. We went into action as never before. Day and night; night and day.

"The closing night of the Seattle Class came at this moment. Then the Great Goddess of Liberty said: 'I want you to rejoice with Me . . . The unfortunate individual in Europe has failed in his attempt to release destruction. Please rejoice in that, and *you have your beloved Saint Germain largely to thank for it.*' (tremendous applause, audience rising!)" (pp. 2-3, Oct. 12, 1938, G. L.)

But despite all this decreeing and the destruction of the "War Entity of the World," the undeclared wars of Europe went right along, and blood-ridden Spain was in the throes of one of the worst civil wars in history.

There was reportedly, however, in the press a sort of

lull during the early part of 1939, which no doubt gave the newspaper-reading "Saint Germain" courage to come forth on February 26, 1939, at the Oakland class, to say:

"You will rejoice with me tonight in knowing that for the present, things are under control in Europe." (p. 3, March 18, 1939, g. l.)

Unfortunately, however, for Saint Germain's witless remark and the peace of Europe, fifteen days later Hitler took Czechoslovakia, and shortly thereafter Mussolini took Albania!

But that of course isn't all of this wretched deception.

One year and two months after this "War Entity of the World" had been consumed (!) and the peace of Europe "saved" by "Saint Germain" and his bands of decreeing I AM-ers, Hitler made his historic onslaught on Poland, and the really big war in Europe was on.

But did the start of the great war in Europe show to the Ballard students the futility of their decrees and reveal to them this great "Master" deception of the age?

It did not! Having failed to keep both small and big wars out of Europe, they are, nevertheless, busily engaged day and night in keeping war out of America!

In fact, they have already "saved" America. Mrs. Ballard in her radio talk at Los Angeles on the afternoon of December 31, 1939, said:

"We have given out these decrees eighteen and twenty hours each day for the protection of America. If we had not, America would be in the same chaos of war that Spain is today."

Since the destruction and parceling of Poland, the wars in Europe have increased in intensity as well as in geographical magnitude. Denmark, Norway, Holland, Belgium went under the iron heel of the Dictator of Europe, and France was soon to meet the greatest humiliation any courageous nation was ever made to suffer.

Where was "Saint Germain" and his mighty army of

"Ascended Masters" the week of June 10, 1940, when war was raging near the gates of Paris and oncoming Nazi tanks were spurting their hell of fire? Where was the *"Great Divine Director,"* he who boasted that "ten of the Ascended Masters could wipe out all armies of the earth"? (p. 5, Nov., 1937, v.) Where was Saint Germain's blessed child, *"Lotus,"* his "Little Dynamite," the reincarnated "JOAN OF ARC," Saviour of France?

Why didn't she save France in 1940 as did the *real* Joan of Arc in 1429?

The present Joan — the one *"who would never be burned at the stake"*—in her luxurious hotel apartment, remained wisely silent about the matter, and after permitting her beloved France to fall, contented herself with the "saving" of her beloved America!

The Ballard "War Entity" is dead, dead as can be, yet Europe today is involved in the greatest and most destructive war of history. What utter insanity it is for these people to claim that they have "saved" America when we today face the menace of the totalitarian powers of Europe and Asia. How dangerous it is for these people to fool great numbers of people into depending upon the false security and protective power of their ridiculous decrees, and ignoring or belittling *real* preparedness to face the enemies to our freedom.

Consciously, or unconsciously, these American-born dictators have played into the hands of the dictators of Europe and Asia.

CHAPTER 23

THOSE BAD BLACK MAGICIANS

We shall now recount how the two Ballards almost single-handedly rid the country of all its black magicians. Of course, they were aided in this by the "Ascended Masters" and their decreeing bands of students; but it is doubtful if this attacking army of black magicians would have been rendered *hors de combat* had it not been for the hard-working "Accredited Messengers of Saint Germain."

For five long years the Ballards have been busily engaged in removing black magicians from America and Europe. The original number of these rather nebulous workers of iniquity was never definitely stated, but they seemed to have been paired about fifty-fifty with the "Ascended Masters."

Chaining them up, or "withdrawing" them from the earth, seems to have been the usual course of procedure; but as some of the more powerful ones, it appears, would somehow get right back into circulation again, these would sometimes have to be "consumed" or "destroyed" by well-directed Light Rays.

Some of these big, bad black magicians have even been known to play boyish pranks upon the "Ascended Masters"! Said Ascended-Master Saint Germain, on September 3, 1938, at the Oakland class: " . . . Secretly there has been spread in your vicinity an activity which pretends to be the Real Activity of Myself . . . The black magician who has his claws upon it is *representing himself to be Me*." (p. 30, Oct., 1938, v., our italics.)

It must, indeed, have been most disconcerting to Saint Germain, and even a stain upon his reputation, to have some evil black magician masquerading as himself!

Then again, how can his students tell *which* "Saint Germain" they have gotten hold of, when they make the "call"—the black-magician Saint Germain or the Ballard Saint Germain?

It is not to be wondered at, therefore, that for a number of years the Ballards and their "Ascended Masters" have been trying to remove these black magicians from circulation.

The method of killing them off, or otherwise making way with them, however, has certain difficulties; for we are told by the "Mighty Astrea" himself, who should know, that *"those individuals always have PHYSICAL BODIES"!* (p. 139, A. M. L., our italics and caps.)

Surely, this complicates the matter, for it would appear to be in conflict with the laws of our land to kill these evil doers who have physical bodies, or otherwise "remove" them without fair and proper trial.

Nevertheless, these Ballard "Masters," either not realizing, or, ignoring, that our American Constitution guarantees fair and impartial trial even to confessed crimnals, have, reportedly, removed or "consumed" hundreds of them.

Even when mandates of the law have to be carried out, the State appoints legally-constituted individuals to take care of the matter. Killing by all others, even by "Ascended Masters," is frowned upon by our Government, and the penalties run high.

At any rate, whatever the legal status of the question may be concerning this wholesale removal of black magicians who have physical bodies, the Ballards and their "Saint Germain" decided to remove these evil doers from circulation.

So, at various classes throughout the country, they reported to their applauding students the latest results of this clean-up of black magicians, who were *"chained,"* *"bound,"* *"consumed,"* *"taken from the atmosphere of earth,"* or otherwise rendered harmless to law-abiding citizens.

Sometimes only *one;* sometimes as many as *five;* and once the report was *nine* removed at one time; which latter seems to have been the record in America.

In Europe, as might be expected, the score runs higher; as many as *thirty* being removed in one day.

Thus, gradually, but surely, the black magicians of the land were decimated; until at last on one memorable occasion at Washington, D. C., scene of Guy Ballard's former labors as "George Washington," Saint Germain gave forth the joyous news that *"all but 12 of the black magicians in the United States had been seized and removed."* (p. 1, Dec. 20, 1938, G. L.)

The ranks of the once powerful army of black magicians in the U. S. A. had been mowed down to a mere handful!

And, not to be wondered at, the audience went wild at such good news, the official report saying: "We leaped to our feet in a tremendous outburst of applause and joyous enthusiasm."

But the Ascended Masters accept no half-way measures. The scattered and tattered army of black magicians was to be completely annihilated.

Taking their cue perhaps from Exodus 22:18, "Thou shalt not suffer a witch to live," it was applied with proper effect to the equally obnoxious "black magician."

So "decreeing students," with victory now almost in sight, continued with even more emotional power and vocal force than before to "work on" these last remaining twelve.

It was in historic Philadelphia, city of our constitutional liberties, that another milestone was reached.

The Archangel Michael himself (!), wielder of the "Sword of Blue Lightning," reported on November 15, 1938, that "5 of the remaining 12 black magicians in the United States had been seized and removed, leaving only 7." (p. 1, Dec. 30, 1938, G. L.)

But it was in little old New York that the most effective blow of all was struck. And, quite properly, "Saint Germain" had the honor of announcing it:

"Praises be!" said he, like a happy school boy, *"the remaining 7 black magicians in the United States have been seized!"* (p. 1, Dec. 30, 1938, G. L.)

According to official report, the effect of this announcement was tremendous:

"The audience jumped to its feet. A tremendous wave of applause broke loose, which carried on and on! . . . Never again would a black magician have activity in America."

But despite these outstanding victories in America, the students were warned that there were still black magicians operating in other parts of the world, and were urged not to let up on their decreeing.

It is not surprising, therefore, that a little later the report came through of some really commendable work in mowing down these last remaining foreigners among the black magicians.

We quote the official report of the Oakland class:

"When the Class began, there were still remaining on earth, principally in Europe, 36 black magicians.

"We determined as never before to call, call, and call to the Great Ones and the Goddess of Light to seize and remove every one of those vicious fiends by the end of the Class.

"To our joy one night Saint Germain said that *all but 6 had been removed!*

" . . . We went into action in our call again.

"Then the Goddess of Light, two days before the end

of the Class, said that *all but one had been removed;* and this last one had been surrounded in his lair by a Wall of Blue Flame thru which he could not pass . . . "

Thus, *"surrounded in his lair,"* the days of this most persistent of all the black magicians on earth seemed numbered.

And sure enough, two days later, right on schedule at the closing night of the class, the great "Goddess of Light" came forth to report that *this last remaining black magician who had been caught in his lair had been completely "withdrawn from the earth!"*

"We leaped to our feet," continues the official report of the victory, "as a mighty ovation swept the Municipal Auditorium. It kept on and on." (pp. 1-2, March 18, 1939, G. L.)

Now that this most stubborn black magician and all the others, both foreign and domestic, have been removed or exterminated, we might think the earth would be a better place on which to live.

But it seems not so. Wars have followed rumors of wars, and strife, pestilence, flood, hurricane, catastrophe, and blitzkriegs have been our lot since the removal of these black magicians.

Yet the "hurling forth" of those marvelous "decrees" continues with unabated force, for it appears there are still other things to be accomplished by these students in order to make the world safe for the "Mighty I AM."

CHAPTER 24

HARBINGERS OF DISASTER

The two heroic and self-proclaimed Messengers of Saint Germain and the Ascended Host have not come into the world to bring olive branches of peace to an already distraught world. Rather have these two come to stir the prophetic waters into new currents and whirlpools of disaster.

They have brought forth in glittering array such a procession of astral ghosts, demons, entities, black magicians, male and female, that all other time-honored processions of headless horsemen and sheeted ghosts have been relegated to the background.

When astral entities pop out from behind every antique, when danger lurks in a little bit of garlic, when the coastal regions of our land are only held in place by shouting bands of I AM-ers, when black magicians are tied up only to get loose again, and so on and on in ever-widening circles of disaster, then we may well suspect that the story tellers and writers are at it again.

Therefore, as we record some of the Ballard prophecies of cataclysms that threaten to destroy some of our American cities and the earth itself, we hope the reader will not take them too seriously. We merely take them out for a much needed airing and sunning, and then we shall let them fly away like eider down in the wind.

Early in their movement the Ballards began to appreciate the psychological effect of holding over the heads of their people the threat of some cataclysm which would destroy the particular city in which the credulous students were living. Like a sword of Damocles, this cataclysm was suspended, as it were, by only a hair, and withheld solely by the heroic efforts of the "Ascended Masters" and their earth-plane "Messengers."

So as the Ballards traveled from city to city, they pictured to their audiences the doom which was in store for a certain city unless sufficient numbers in that city would join the decreeing army of Mighty I AM-ers and shout commands to the "Ascended Masters." It seems that these great "Beings" would pay no attenion to humanity's woes unless they were shouted at and ordered around.

If sufficient numbers of students would only take part in this decree-shouting, these "Masters" and their Messengers would not only save the world from the big, bad wolf, the *black magician*, and from *wars* which still go on, but they would also keep miscellaneous and sundry *"Gas Belts"* from hurling mankind to destruction.

At Washington, D. C., on the evening of December 8, 1938, "Saint Germain," as is his usual happy duty, came forth to praise the work of his Messengers, but this time he tells the appreciative audience how they saved the city from destruction.

"These two whom I love so much," he said, "who have given such implicit obedience, are as humble as humbleness can be . . . Without them mankind would have been in the most seething vortex of war right in your midst today. Your Capital would not be here today!" (p. 6, Dec., 1938, v.)

At New York, on October 8, 1937, they had none other than the *"Lord Maitreya,"* who had formerly been a Master connected with the Theosophical Society but who had now assertedly embraced the Mighty I AM, say:

"You stand with the war entity above you and the destructive gas belts beneath." (p. 160, A. M. L.)

Poor New York! Besieged from above and below, there seemed little hope for her; but a little later, at their next visit to the apparently doomed city, the "Goddess of

Peace" gave the New Yorkers a breath of hope.

"Our Records show great devastation has already been prevented in your land . . . Your city where you rest so serenely tonight would not have been here the past eighteen months, if it had not been for the call to Light." (Page 11, July, 1938, v.)

San Francisco, if we can believe it, has been saved a number of times by the Ballards and their local I AM-ers.

"Before the Messengers came," said Saint Germain in August, 1937, "your city was in great danger." (p. 3, September, 1937, v.) And on every subsequent visit he would give additional warnings about "Gas Belts" alleged to lie underneath the city.

However, they overdid it a bit here, and the San Francisco wide-awake Chamber of Commerce came down on their heads.

It was all on account of a mimeograph letter sent by the Ballards to the faithful at the San Francisco "I AM Sanctuary." We quote:

"Saint Germain says that San Francisco is in greater danger of earthquake than any city in the whole United States because of the gas underlying it. San Francisco's WHOLE PROTECTION rests in the guard of the I AM students at the SANCTUARY . . . All sincere students are asked to stand by the SANCTUARY which is the Light's Protection in San Francisco against another earthquake."

The Ballards, well aware that the "Sanctuary" in San Francisco was having considerable internal disturbance at this time, evidently took this method of holding it together, making it appear that the fate of the city depended upon the unified work of the I AM-ers there. What public spirited citizen among the San Francisco I AM-ers *wouldn't* bury his differences to save the city!

It seems that the faithful at the Sanctuary actually did take this danger very much to heart, buried the hatchet, and, in an endeavor to "save" the city, wide publicity was given to this letter. At least so it appears from a newspaper article in the *San Francisco Examiner* on May 28, 1938, headed: "C. OF C. PUTS 'MASTER' WISE ON PROPHECY." We quote in part:

"Nasty little rumors to the effect that the Chamber of Commerce has put the fix on none other than 'The Ascended Master St. Germain' got themselves considerable credence yesterday . . . "He speaks or writes through his only accredited messengers, Mr. and Mrs. G. W. Ballard . . . A lot of Bay region cash goes into their pockets."

This newspaper article went on to quote Saint Germain's dire predictions about San Francisco's over-supply of gas. Then a subtitle headed, "DELETE-QUAKE," said:

"Evidence that Saint Germain had been seen by the C. of C., or somebody, was found when a *revised* version of the same mimeograph sheet emanated from the local 'sanctuary.' The new screed is identical in every paragraph with the old, except that the word 'earthquake' is out . . ."

That is what comes of having a wide-awake Chamber of Commerce in a city which is sufficiently sensitive about its "Gas Belts" as to have the nerve to put the "fix" on even the great Ascended Master Saint Germain!

Los Angeles, as might be expected, has also been "saved" many times. But unlike San Francisco, its Chamber of Commerce has not yet put the "fix" on the Ascended Master Saint Germain. Perhaps the local Chamber of Commerce believes any kind of publicity for good old Los Angeles has good advertising value, and that tourists will come out to the land of sunshine to see bumper crops of heterodoxy just as readily as bumper crops of anything else.

But we do think the C. of C., or somebody, should call a halt on Saint Germain's *"tidal waves"* and *"destructive Light Rays from Russia"* sweeping in to destroy the city.

On New Year's Day in 1936, speaking at Los Angeles, "Saint Germain" said that the call of the students had rendered a tremendous service.

" . . . It has prevented a tidal wave striking the western coast which was thought would have come into action the second of January, 1936." And he rightly adds:

"How much more wonderful it is that mankind might be enjoying the Tournament of Roses than to be in the throes of a destructive activity." (p. 12, Feb., 1936, v.)

A couple of years later he again saved the city, this time from a *"destructive Ray"* assertedly directed from a "focus in the Ural mountains between Russia and Siberia."

"Had I not been able to check this attempt," he says, "there would have been no Shrine Class in July! because there would not have been any place to have it!" (p. 3, Feb. 18, 1938, G. L.)

Thus from city to city the Ballards traveled, and wherever they went, they told the story of the "Ascended Masters" or their "Accredited Messengers" saving that city from destruction. There was always a convenient gas belt, tidal wave, or destroying "Ray" to bring forth if the people did not evidence sufficient interest in the Mighty I AM.

"Tremendous protection has been given the coasts of America!" said the Ballards to students in cities which would be affected by the disaster. And to enforce obedience, they shrewdly added: "Do you want to undo that, beloved students everywhere, and let this cataclysm come forth and destroy all . . . ?" (p. 38, March, 1937, v.)

In their travels, they came across, one day, a leaflet telling the story of an alleged vision of General Washington received during his Valley Forge encampment, which was entitled: *"General Washington's Vision."* The story was told by a feeble, old man of ninety-nine years, who said Washigton told it to him.

The substance of the vision was: "Three great perils would come upon the Republic . . . the most fearful being the third . . . and that help would come in the shape of

Divine Assistance."

Immediately, the Ballards began to refer to the "great peril," for it seems that Saint Germain had not told them before of this danger confronting the Nation, and the memory of the present reincarnated George Washington (!) failed to recall so important an event until this story of a ninety-nine-year-old man came into his hands.

Their numerous "Gods" and "Goddesses" soon got the idea of the "Vision," too, and made the most of it.

At New York, the "Silent Watcher" said:

" . . . Should the third episode in Washington's vision take place in your America, there would scarcely be enough people left on the earth to make one small city." (p. 121, A. M. L.)

At West Palm Beach, the "Goddess of Liberty" said:

" . . . The third episode has been the greatest danger confronting mankind today. If it swept into America, the whole world would be a seething vortex of destruction." (p. 5, Jan., 1938, v.)

Such were some of the forebodings of doom made by these harbingers of disaster as they traveled from city to city. They injected needless fear into the minds of credulous people, and deluded them through promises of Ascended Master protection to join the army of Mighty I AM-ers.

Military armies were said by the great Napoleon to travel on their stomachs, but this "I AM" army of Saint Germain's has been nourished on the pabulum of disaster. The whole thing is an outstanding instance of the use of fear psychology, wherein weird processions of phantom masters, black magicians, astral entities, and other hobgoblins are made to pass in disordered review before the minds of their followers.

Some day their credulous students will awaken as from a trance and recognize it all as the absurd delusion and unreality that it is.

CHAPTER 25

SEX TEACHINGS OF BALLARDISM

The Ballard cult with its distorted and fanatical view of sex has been a prolific cause of divorce and unhappiness among its members, and has produced widespread repercussions among non-members.

Sex, according to the Ballards and their "Ascended Masters," is absolutely taboo except for procreative purposes, and even then they definitely discourage their members from bringing children into the world. The "Ascension," they say, is too near for that.

To properly take care of the ever-growing sex and marriage problems among their students the Ballards brought forth a new "lady Ascended Master" and called her the "Goddess of Purity." The "Goddess" thinks that I AM-ers, all and sundry, should get off the earth by making their "Ascension" instead of settling down and rearing families—a sort of race suicide of the elect. Let the others go through all the trouble and bother of raising families. The Goddess wants none of it. Says she:

"... Those of today who have the opportunity and the privilege of gaining their Freedom from human bondage through their Ascension, should certainly not contemplate sex or family relationship in that respect. You have served a long time in raising children, in exercising undesirable sex force. Is it not time now that you might forget it for a few years ... ? There will still be enough of mankind left to take care of the requirements of birth ... You cannot seek another for the desire of sex and expect yourself to be free!" (pp. 25-26, Nov., 1939, v.)

Despite the thumbs-down attitude on marriage and the rearing of children the Ballard cult goes in strongly for what they call *"Twin Rays."* It must be explained that this has nothing whatever to do with ordinary twins or quintuplets, but presents the idea that each person is but *half* a human being—that somewhere in space is his other half, wandering, as it were, like a loosened planetoid from the part from which it was broken.

That is the deplorable condition the general run of humanity is in today, it seems, but the Ascended Masters and a few of the lucky I AM-ers have recovered their lost "halves" and are presumably living blissful lives together.

The "Accredited Messengers" of the Ascended Master Saint Germain are quite naturally one of those lucky couples, each being the Twin Ray of the other. Saint Germain himself has informed them that this is so.

Their book, *The Magic Presence,* is full of the Twin Ray idea, the lady and gentlemen Ascended Masters and young couples in it being paired off, for the most part, into blissful unions of Twin Rays.

In this book, along with Saint Germain's other strenuous duties, he is revealed as a sort of Twin Ray specialist. Though peculiarly never mentioning his own Twin Ray, he can spot the Twin Rays of others most unerringly, and makes it his special Ascended-Master duty to draw the young people together and tell them about the laws of love, marriage, and romance.

This all reads well in the Ballard story books (albeit a bit too heavenly for plain-thinking earth beings), but the sad fact remains that most of the Ballard students in the outer world do not know where their other "half" is. Saint Germain, it seems, is the *only* Ascended Master who is able to tell them—and he talks only through Guy and Edna Ballard. The students, therefore, must get all their information concerning 50% of themselves from two human beings who also have a large and growing option on the other 50%.

It is sometimes difficult for the Ballards to remember who-is-who in this Twin Ray business, and Guy Ballard at least one time in his Messianic career made a deep and tragic error.

It seems that he had informed two of his favorite staff members that they were Twin Rays; and this, as usual, came from the great Saint Germain, the Twin Ray specialist, himself.

However, a little later on, the *"Great Divine Director,"* not being a specialist in this particular field and perhaps forgetful of what brother Saint Germain had said, severely startled a little group of staff members and students one evening by saying that *ALL* the staff members' Twin Rays had ascended and were not to be found on the earth plane.

That was a most grievous slip for a *Perfect Being* to make, and it had the result, among other things, of getting one of the "halves" of the combination out of the movement; and then Saint Germain had to inform the other remaining "half" that he had to choose between the *"Light of God that Never Fails"* and his wife. The gentleman wisely chose the latter, and so as a result of the Great Divine Director's slip the Ballard organization lost both of Saint Germain's favorite Twin Rays.

Twin Rays today in the Ballard organization are almost as scarce as quintuplets. Even Donald Eros Ballard is without his Twin Ray on the earth plane ("Saint Germain" told him so)—a little matter which must have been fully realized by his wife in her recent divorce suit against him.

As a result of an apparent scarcity of Twin Rays among duly wedded I AM-ers, one or both of the partners may be inclined to look for some imaginary Twin Ray or Rays out in space somewheres. And sometimes it has not been an imaginary "Twin Ray" on some heavenly sphere either, but some ecstatic earth love on this very mundane sphere. All of which is quite understandable in this weird cult which teaches that each I AM-er is only *half* an I AM-er, the other "half" being somewhere else—and may not at all be the present spouse.

But the Twin Ray idea is not the only reason for so many divorces among I AM-ers. Far from it. Complete abolition of sex is taught by this cult, and although they formerly taught that sex could be used to bring children into the world, they today teach quite differently. As we have seen from the Goddess of Purity's (?) statement, a philosophy of race suicide is preached. No marriage, no children. Make the "Ascension" instead. Leave the earth to the morons. *What a wonderful chance for the Dictators!*

Despite the alleged "purity" of this cult, a disguised but easily discernable *eroticism* plays through this cult.

Guy Ballard, over and over again on the public platform, referred to his so-called "Sex Law," and seemed to take delight in picturing the fearful consequences which would result for any violation of it. At one of his early classes in Los Angeles (August 19, 1935), he said:

"The sex urge was only to be used for procreation. When it is used for so-called pleasure, mankind loses the dominion of his physical form . . . When it is wasted, the body becomes decrepit and helpless . . . Your aura becomes charged with the most vicious entities you can imagine."

Since then, with fanatical persistence, the Ballards have constantly referred to the subject of sex. They inject the strongest sort of fear-thought into the minds of their students should any violation of their instruction take place. Time and again their "Ascended Masters" come forth to keep this subject flaming before the minds of their audiences.

" . . . To seek these classes," says their Great Divine Director, "to gain acquaintance and companionship for sex desire is the most infamous thing ever on this earth! . . .

There are those who have been doing it . . . If you don't stop it, I shall pick you out! . . . You have been told repeatedly that unless you cease your sex desire, you cannot gain your Freedom and Ascension . . . Do not be surprised if I release the Fire, the Flame of Life to burn these desires out of you tonight. (applause)" (pp. 18-19, April, 1940, v.)

This sex taboo teaching has been given indiscriminately in public for over five years among people of all walks of life. It applies, they say, to all regardless of their circumstances, conditions, beliefs, obligations, spirituality, or anything else. It is the unalterable, inexorable "Law of Sex," and will react upon all who disobey it, producing degeneration of both mind and body.

Naturally, such extreme views concerning the dominant, biological urge of sex, enunciated to people who in their marital lives had built up certain habits in regard to it, had widespread repercussions.

This sex teaching alone has resulted in an extraordinary number of divorces, separations, and disagreements among married people, many of whom up to the time Ballardism entered their homes had doubtless been living normal, sensible sex lives.

With the sudden introduction of a fanatical religion into the home environment, with its rigid taboo of sex expression in any form, a condition of affairs was brought about which frequently became intolerable to the marriage partner who did not embrace the religious fanaticism of the other partner.

The result was separation or divorce in many homes which had formerly been happy and contented ones before the arrival of Ballardism and its extreme sex teaching. The instructions from the Ballards were to divorce the partner who desired marital relations, or leave the movement.

Referring to the unhappiness that has come to the I AM

students as a result of this sex teaching, the Great Divine Director encourages them to go on with the program, even though it separates husband and wife, parent and child.

"I say to you blessed ladies of the Light," says he, "be not dismayed in the unhappiness that has come of your search for and acceptance of the Light. Stand firm and unyielding . . . Everyone of you must now stand by your 'I AM Presence'—I don't care how much you love your wives, husbands and children . . . If your home life has become unbearable and you have severed it, don't seek the companionship of other men . . . Ungratified sex desires will make a human being the most vicious individual ever known . . . " (pp. 21-22, April, 1940, v.)

But sex was not the only thing which broke up these homes. The general philosophy itself, with its devotion to "Masters," fanatical inhibitions and prohibitions, caused and is causing today many intolerable conditions in the home environment, separating life-long partners and estranging children and relatives.

Decrees which have to be uttered the live-long day and half the night leave little time to devote to the duties and obligations of home building. Children are neglected, the husband or wife ignored, for this newer and more thrilling experiment of worshiping unseen "Masters" and "Goddesses."

A marriage partner who before the advent of Ballardism was all that the other could reasonably expect, almost overnight became neglectful of things which had produced happiness in the past in a fanatical endeavor to follow this newer and more streamlined pathway to happiness.

All this, and much more than we have space to record, is the result of this teaching—in a land which the Ballards assertedly came to "Save."

Further, much of the alleged "purity" and "morality" of this cult is puritanical and ridiculous. This is readily seen from the following quotations.

A "gentleman Ascended Master" who goes by the name of "Wondrous Harmony," is responsible for the following gem of thought:

"Married ladies and married gentlemen," admonished this disturbed gentleman, "if you want to save yourselves grave danger, *do not go anywhere alone with each other for any reason whatsoever!*" (p. 10, June, 1939, v., our italics.)

That was actually printed in the Ballard official magazine! And "Wondrous Harmony," warming up to his subject, continued by saying:

"No married woman has a right to go with another man that is married. No married man has a right to go with a woman who is married and be with them except to transact business, and then *only in the presence of others.*" (p. 10, our italics.)

That is surely definite enough, but it *would* look sort of silly to have to call in a chaperon to be present during business deals with members of the opposite sex.

The Twin Ray specialist, just as puritanical in thought as the Ascended Master "Wondrous Harmony," on June 28, 1938, spoke to the members of the Ballard staff as follows:

"I ask in all kindness that no one of the staff take any other married or unmarried man or woman to dinner alone. No matter how innocent the individuals are, there are spies acting everywhere . . . There can't be anything hidden from me—I know every motive and desire!"

The young people in particular are warned against the slightest expression of affection, however innocent, with members of the opposite sex.

"Remember," says the Simon-pure Saint Germain to the boys and girls assembled at the class at Los Angeles on April 4, 1937, "you can love your friends more powerfully without your arms around them." (p. 270, A. M. D.)

And Sanat Kumara, another Ballard "Master," who hails paradoxically from the traditional planet of love, Venus, says: "The greatest mistake of mankind today is to think that they must have physical contact in order to express love." (p. 8, Aug., 1938, v.)

The two Ballards themselves in a special plea to the "Young People of America" say: "We ask ALL under this Radiation to stop all practices of what the world calls necking, kissing and hugging those of the opposite sex who are not your own relatives." (p. 33, Aug., 1938, v.)

To every good or bad rule, however, there seem to be always exceptions, even among Ascended Masters and Accredited Messengers, for the "Great Divine Director" in his great wisdom has said:

"Oh dear hearts, our beloved Messengers have stood forth before the world; and if they feel the impulse to put their arms around a man or woman to give encouragement, they do it!" (p. 15, April, 1937. v.)

Even Saint Germain, despite his latter-day puritanism, is not altogether lacking in affectional responses. On August 30, 1936, at the class in San Francisco, he came forth on the stage (at least Guy Ballard said he did), and among other flattering remarks about the smiling but unblushing Lotus, said:

"This Blessed One here—your Little Dynamite—I have always held her in My Embrace of Light, many times in My Tangible Form—in My Tangible Embrace of Light."

And feeling a good response from the audience, he added: "Do you notice how sort of chummy we are today? It is wonderful!" (p. 13, Oct., 1936, v.)

Nevertheless, despite these little occasional personal laxities and tolerances distributed properly among their membership, the "Ascended Masters" are generally most insistent and fanatical in their instructions to the married, unmarried, and would-be married. Their students are held under the spotlight of strict disciplinarianism, with the Ascended Masters and Messengers claiming to know all that is going on within their lives.

One of the reasons for such puritanical sex teachings seems rather obvious.

In the failures of the average student to fulfill these sex admonitions in all particulars, the Ballards have a perfect alibi for the non-deliverance of their promised miracles. For the reason why these poor struggling students do not make their "Ascension," have their "financial freedom," achieve "radiant health," and so on, is they have not kept sufficient "emotional control" over their feelings!

Knowing their weaknesses, these students blame themselves instead of the Ballards for the non-appearance of promised miracles; and so the stress and struggle of killing out the "entity-demons" within themselves—which they are assured are responsible for their backsliding—still continues.

What complexes are built up, what mental and physical reactions are brought about by such teachings, only time and an intimate investigation into their lives will reveal.

But certainly within the lives of students who go to such fanatical extremes, there are queer tangles of suppressed desires . . . "Twin Ray" complexes . . . condemnation of self or marriage partner for not being able to live up to the idea of a non-sexual love . . . lurking fear of alleged mental and physical degeneration as a result of giving in to the dominant biological urge . . . the spectre of divorce or separation . . . and dozens of other reactions from such ill-advised and distorted sex teachings.

There is consequently a sad need for a sane consideration of the sex question among the Ballard students, a real need for the psychoanalyst and psychiatrist to straighten out the tangles in the lives of these people.

CHAPTER 26

SOME RESULTS OF BALLARDISM

Probably in no other movement has there ever been such attempt at widespread interference with the personal lives of its members as in this cult of the Mighty I AM.

The Ballard students are instructed to push people out of their lives who cannot embrace the Mighty I AM teachings, and to have as little as possible to do with them. As a result, the deepest relationships of many years' standing have been severed by zealous students fanatical enough to live up to the Ballard instructions.

Husband, wife, mother, or some other relative living in a fanatical Mighty I AM family, has actually been kept in another part of the house and denied former privileges because he or she would not embrace the Ballard doctrines. We cite an instance of this in the following story.

A car was parked outside of an "I AM Temple" in a certain city. The man within it had his head bowed over the steering wheel.

Another man was waiting outside this same "I AM" meeting place, and was pacing back and forth.

In passing by the parked car this latter man noticed that the man with head bowed over the wheel was sobbing. In ready comprehension, he approached him.

"I see they've got you, too," he said.

The man at the wheel raised himself up confusedly, quickly brushing the tears away. Then seeing the understanding in the other's face, said:

"Yes, I was conceded an unusual privilege today. I ate at the table with my wife and children for the first time in weeks. They've had me in another part of the house."

He looked pathetically into the face of the other man who seemed to understand, and added:

"I hope other privileges will be conceded too, or at least these same ones continued, but one never knows what the demand will be next. I am waiting to take my family home."

This intolerance of the other person's beliefs and methods of living is a direct outcome of the Ballard teachings, particularly among so-called "hundred per cent students" who follow the Ballard instructions in every way.

We quote the following letter written by a former class leader under date of June 29, 1939:

"Last July during the Shrine class I had a private interview with Mrs. Ballard, at which time she told me (I might well use the terms, *ordered* or *commanded*, as that was her manner) to call for the release of my own mother, whom she knew I love with all my heart, just as we were taught to call for the release of our little pets.

"Why? Because my mother did not believe in them nor their teaching, though she never opposed me or them in any way.

"Mrs. Ballard told me I was carrying a big load and that my mother was a 'Vampire activity' keeping alive on my energy.

"She shot this question at me: 'Doesn't your mother take a lot of soda?' 'Yes.' Then: 'Doesn't she eat a lot?' I answered: 'She has a good appetite.' 'Yes,' she said, 'and she sits around no good to herself or anyone else and she can keep alive for years drawing on your energy and living on it. *Call for her release, you have work to do!*'

"Then she told me to come home and 'Tell ——— to stop all sex relations.' (——— is my daughter, who is very happily married to a fine fellow and they have two beautiful children.)

"I told her: 'But they want two more children,' etc.

'No,' said the dictator, 'It is too near the Ascension for that now.'

"I asked: 'What if her husband will not agree?' 'Tell her to take a child by each hand and walk out and slam the door,' was her reply."

The Ballards themselves, at least in this regard, evidently live up to their own teaching. Years ago, Mrs. Ballard pushed her own aged mother and only sister out of her life because they would not accept the Mighty I AM or believe that Guy Ballard's books and his trips to India were true, knowing as they did that he was right here in the United States all the while.

Former students who have had the courage to get out of the cult are oftentimes denounced in public and even *decrees for their physical death demanded*.

On Sunday evening, July 3, 1939, at a "Hundred Per Cent Group" in Los Angeles, Guy Ballard spoke the following words, saying they were from the great Ascended Master, "Sanat Kumara."

"Do not again make the call for anyone to return to this Light. Rather call for their *release from those bodies* that they have chosen to desecrate by vicious falsehoods against the Messengers of this Light."

Not only do the Ballards teach their students to call for the "release" of certain individuals from their bodies, but it is their duty, they say, to "*free*" all ANIMALS from their bodies, because: "*Animal forms were created in the beginning by powerful black magicians.*" (p. 22, Oct., 1936, v.) We quote:

" . . . It is the DUTY of every I AM Student to call the Mighty I AM Presence and Ascended Masters to FREE ALL ANIMAL LIFE from its discord, limitation and imperfection." (p. 30, Oct., 1937, v., our capitals.)

To the credit of some of their students, there was a protest against this inhuman doctrine. One of them wrote the Ballard official representative, and received the following reply:

"Now you ask me if it is right to put animals out of their bodies. I am going to answer this by simply telling you what I have heard Mrs. Ballard say—that animal forms are imprisoned life and as you know, we have a decree in our magazine and one in the new decree book sending all animals into the higher life and Light.

"Now, dear, each one of us must interpret that as best we can. *I do know many of the students have put their beloved animals out.*"

The fact that many of these animal pets have been "put out" or "released" is again shown by Guy Ballard's letter to one of the students in November of 1937, dictated and signed by him personally:

"When this call is sincerely made and the desire for their RELEASE is felt in the feelings, it is quickly effective in releasing this life . . . This is accomplished in perfect peace and harmony as has been demonstrated in the case of HUNDREDS of the students. GWB:PBC" (Our capitals.)

In other words, *hundreds* of animal pets have been "released" because the students *decreed their DEATH!*

However, what really happened was admitted by the Ballard representative whose letter was quoted: "Many of the students have put their beloved animals out." The decrees didn't work—so they chloroformed, drowned or otherwise *killed* their trusting little animal friends!

One such case is quoted in the letter below written in November, 1937. It is only one of many cases where fanatical I AM-ers have killed their animal pets. We quote:

"The phone rang this morning and an I AM-er called and told me that another of Mrs. ———'s 100% class was put in a sanitarium last week.

"It seems that she owned a lovely dog and that they were told there were to be no more dogs. She had the dog electrocuted.

"Her family resented it so they had her taken to a psychiatrist who analyzed her and of course she did not know when to speak and of what to speak, and started in on the books, and when she was asked why she did not give the dog to ————, she said, it was just as bad for him to have it as it was for her.

"Well, they pronounced her insane and put her away last week. God pity them all."

Some additional results of the Ballard doctrines may be summed up in a few short sentences.

It has taught credulous followers to forget everything else but the "Mighty I AM," tending to hold its people in moronic ignorance of what is going on in the world.

It has caused fanatical students to "decree" long hours during the day and part of the night, with such intensity and emotionalism that a number of them have had nervous breakdowns, or have been confined to psychopathic wards and insane asylums.

It has produced untold mental suffering from fears of catacylsms, entities, black magicians, destructive decrees, and other fear-inspiring bogeys.

It has caused students to worship at the shrines of an endless number of mythological gods and heathenish "Masters," instead of teaching a devotion to the One and True God, the Creator of the Universe, of whose grandeur, love, and wisdom there is no end.

It has induced some of its fanatical devotees to get rid of their life insurance, thinking that they or their loved ones would soon make their "Ascension" and have no need of it.

It has promised financial security by merely "decreeing" it, which resulted in some of their people quitting their jobs, turning over their savings to the Ballards, and neglecting their financial future.

It has caused people to neglect their physical health

as a result of being told that it was not necessary to seek diversions, play games, exercise, or place any dependence in physical remedies.

It has brought about needless deaths because of dependence upon "Ascended Masters" and "decrees" to restore health, remove tumors, etc., instead of sanely instituting physical and surgical treatment when necessary.

It has produced in the student a false sense of the greatness of the little personal self, which is the self which makes its decrees to the "Mighty I AM," causing distortion of the real truth concerning the God consciousness within.

It has caused the student to look outside of himself for guidance to some invisible "Teacher" or psychic "Master" whose real purposes and designs are of the nature of things hidden, and whose responsibility and honesty may be nil.

It has produced in the minds of many people the idea that animals have been created by "black magicians" instead of by God, causing in these cases a severance of the beautiful relationship which has always existed between the dog and his master, and a breaking of man's comradeship with other members of the animal kingdom.

It has through the hands of fanatical students sent hundreds of little pets to the pound to be killed, or the sensitive animal cruelly sent away from its accustomed home.

It has caused untold grief, insanity, and even *suicide!*

With all these sins and crimes the Ballard "Mighty I AM Instruction of the Ascended Masters" stands indicted, and it is time that the public should know the full truth of it and its history written.

CHAPTER 27

THE ATTACK ON CHRISTIANITY

The Mighty I AM cult of Guy and Edna Ballard will go down in history as one of the most insidious affronts to the religion of the Christ that America has ever seen.

Abroad, we have seen the spectacle of a dictator attempting to do away with religious worship. Christian Americans look with consternation on the burning of church edifices and the confiscation of its symbols of worship. Yet some of these same patriotic and religious Americans, ignore, tolerate, and some even promote one of the most subtle attacks on the Christian church and its teachings that we have ever had in American history.

For five years we have seen two people proclaiming by means of the lecture platform, over the radio, and through their voluminous literature, the strange doctrines embodied in the "Saint Germain Instruction of the Mighty I AM."

In this so-called instruction, a "Mystery Man" of the 18th century has been resurrected or pushed forward, that he might supplant in the hearts of thousands the Christ of Christendom.

Or to curry favor with those who might be inclined to look askance at this sacrilege, the Ballards brought forth an *astral* counterfeit of the Christ to appease those who still hold reverence in their hearts for the Personage who braved the organized power of the Sanhedrin and sought to save the people from idolatrous worship of heathen gods.

And, instead of being satisfied with producing *one*

astral god or "Saint," these "Accredited Messengers of Saint Germain" have given their poor psychologized followers the most multitudinous array of gods and goddesses since the days of heathen mythology.

Not only have these two self-proclaimed "Messengers" endeavored by hypnotic methods to substitute an 18th-century miracle worker for the Man of Galilee and to bring forth a vapid astral creation for those who still want a Christ, but they actually endeavored to personally steal the show from their own psychic creations!

Time and again the writer has sat among the huge assemblage at the Shrine Civic Auditorium in Los Angeles and heard the Ballard smooth-tongue announcer say:

"Dear ones, these blessed Messengers today are occupying the place that Jesus, the Christ, occupied two thousand years ago!"

Not one voice of protest in that audience did he hear against this utterance. Only a placid acceptance, or a look of sickening personality worship, was usually observed on the faces of those present.

On the stages of the various "Temples" and auditoriums where the Ballards lecture there is always shown the painted portrait of the Head of Christ, by Charles Sindelar. Incidentally, Mr. Sindelar is the "Western Representative of the Saint Germain Press," and publisher of the *Voice of the I AM.*

And always, on the stage, alongside of this Christ picture, is a portrait, by the same artist, of the mighty "Ascended Master Saint Germain."

When the Ballards first came to Los Angeles in 1935 bringing only their "Saint Germain" with them, they almost forgot to mention Jesus or say much about Him.

This was soon found to be a mistake. They discovered that many people in Los Angeles, which incidentally has its quota of other Saviors, still wanted the Christ of the Gospels.

The Sindelar Christ head, which had been created previous to their trip to Los Angeles, was therefore extremely timely and most acceptable to the Ballards when it was called to their attention. "Saint Germain" had evidently failed to mention the picture to them before coming to Los Angeles.

Without the Christ, even their most enthusiastic supporters balked at accepting their "Saint." Therefore, the two pictures were, and are today, presented together instead of the Saint alone.

It was, however, an expediency rather than a worshipful necessity that Jesus should come into the Ballard plan of salvation, for their real "Savior" is, was, and shall be, the bearded and mustached, piercing-eyed Saint Germain!

And their followers have gradually learned to accept the substitution.

In the first editions of their books the Ballards printed a cut of what was perhaps the best available picture they could secure which met their ideas of a bearded Master.

But, alas! Saint Germain's beard, mustache, and closely-cropped hair in that picture were all as black as night!

Now, black is supposed by them to be the symbol and color of *black magic,* and that of course wouldn't do in their "dazzling, white-light" Mighty I AM Instruction. So, despite the fact that this particular black-bearded portrait had been okayed by Saint Germain himself and authenticated by them through their own 1934 copyright notice printed below the portrait, something simply had to be done about it.

The fortunate addition of Charles Sindelar, the artist, to the Ballard organization, evidently pointed to them the way out of this dark-visaged predicament. Mr. Sindelar was commissioned by Saint Germain himself—so Guy Ballard said—to paint his own peculiar portrait, who, it appears, despite his noteworthy achievements in "precipitating" Government money, could not paint or precipitate his own picture.

We learn from one of the Ballard advertising leaflets that "Saint Germain revealed himself to Mr. Sindelar previous to and while he was painting Saint Germain's likeness, and he has said that it is splendid"—which assures us that the portrait is now quite authentic!

And so, since that time, the faithful have had a "Saint Germain," far removed from the stigma of being a black magician because of the color of his beard; for he has succumbed to the blondine tendency of the age and has come off Mr. Sindelar's easel a golden-haired, blue-eyed, sandy-mustached Saint!

Having successfully substituted a new Saint Germain portrait for the old one, and an astral creation of Jesus, the Ballards proceeded to discredit the Christian Bible. The students were early urged to substitute the Ballard books for the Bible, this being done by "Jesus" himself.

"I urge students everywhere," said this astral Jesus " . . . *to forget everything else you have ever studied.*" (p. 5, Feb., 1936, v.)

Jesus' own life story, as recorded in the gospels, was to be forgotten, and the Ballard literature substituted instead!

Intent on their idea of substituting the Saint Germain series of books for the Bible and their "Saint Germain" for Jesus, the Ballards brought forth their astral "Jesus" to say:

"It is My Determination to break down within the concepts of Mankind the feeling that Saint Germain should not be accepted as Myself. I shall not give My Radiation to anyone who questions it." (p. 6, Dec., 1937, v.) "I want to say to the whole world: 'Every human being who rejects My Beloved Brother, Saint Germain, rejects Me, and don't forget it.' " (p. 15, Feb., 1937, v.)

This is the same counterfeit "Jesus," who in addition to saying, "*don't forget it,*" would sometimes close his discourse by weakly saying: "*I thank you.*" Imagine it!

Then showing that the Ballards are today doing a

greater work than Jesus did, they had this same astral Jesus say: " . . . The calls of the Messengers are performing thousands more healings than I performed!" (p. 6, Dec., 1937, v.)

Thus for the I AM student, Jesus and the Christian Bible are both discredited, and are being supplanted by Saint Germain and his series of books.

The Christian ideology of the worship of One God through His divine Messenger, the Christ, is being replaced by a blasphemous and fantastic lot of astral gods and goddesses who are supposed to propitiate the sins of the I AM students.

The ideal of a loving God, Creator of the Universe, whose Power and Glory are without end, is being taken over by a fictitious "Mighty I AM Presence" located from twelve to fifty feet overhead, floating around like a balloon and connected with the physical body below by means of a thread of light substance.

It is this creation that the Ballard students *shout at* when they go through their decree antics. All of which recalls to mind the prophecy of the Christ of nineteen hundred years ago:

"For there shall arise false Christs, and false prophets, and shall show great signs and wonders; so as to lead astray, if possible, even the elect. Behold, I have told you beforehand." (Matthew 24:24-25.)

Demonstrating before his group what he thought of the Bible, one of the prominent I AM leaders flung it down upon the platform and stamped upon it.

Despite all their irreverence for Christ and the Bible, the Ballards actually made an effort to build up a following among church people; and in so doing made use of the crudest and dizziest sales psychology. They resurrected some of the most revered characters of the Bible and had them advertise the Ballards and boost their book sales.

For any Protestants who might be attracted by the

bait, they brought forth Jesus' most beloved disciple, "John the Beloved," and had him do his bit in advertising and proselyting. We quote: " . . . There never were two such interested, selfless human beings on the face of this earth as the Messengers are." (p. 13, Feb., 1938, v.)

For the Roman Catholics who might be lured away because of the "*Saint*" prefix to St. Germain's name—which they always insist upon writing out in full—they brought forth the "Virgin Mary," and had her say nice things about the "Ascended Masters" and the Ballard advertising leaflets:

"The inception of the Catholic Church," says the Virgin Mary (!) "was brought about by and through the Power of the Ascended Masters"—their own, of course, there are no others. (p. 426, A. M. L.) "These little 'Save America Folders' which the blessed ones have sent forth . . . are doing tremendous things. Keep it up, I urge you!" (p. 434.)

The Ballards actually told their audiences that Cardinal Bonzano, during the Eucharistic Congress held June, 1936, at Soldiers' Field, Chicago, *made his ascension!*

When it was called to their attention that Cardinal Bonzano *did not die until a year and five months later,* and at *Rome* instead of Chicago, Guy Ballard made the following absurd effort to cover up the fabrication:

"What of it?" he asked. "Certainly He did!" and went on to say:

"While the physical body remained during those months, yet it was but a shell, and the Ascension was accomplished there at that time." (p. 29, Aug., 1939, v.)

Can one imagine anything more absurd than the representative of the Pope going around for seventeen months attending to the exactitudes of his official duties when he himself physically was not there—and with only his "shell" officiating? And to force acceptance of this absurdity upon his psychologized students, Ballard said: "Who of you are to say what the Great Law of Life may do?"

The Ballard harvest of souls, however, has been particularly bountiful among the waving fields of the un-
orthodox. Many of these, having no abiding resting place,
spiritually speaking, were attracted by greener fields beyond the old occult barriers.

"The old occult order has been set aside," the Ballards
announced; and so, like the days of the forty-niners, the
"gold rush" was on, both spiritually and materially speaking.

But most of the material gold flowed into the coffers of
the Ballards instead of the other way around. And most of
the spiritual gold today is being found spurious.

From the Theosophists the Ballards purloined their
Masters, and set out to catch their students with unique
psychic holds all their own.

They had the Masters Morya and Kuthumi come forth
to say that when they started the Theosophical Society
through their messenger, Madame Blavatsky, they *"were
not then ascended,"* and *"could only go so far."* (pp. 317
and 334, A. M. L.)

And very generously and humbly these new *"Ascended"* Masters admitted: *"Our Beloved Saint Germain has
accomplished more in three years than We did in the many
years of Our humble efforts."* (p. 323.)

The Ballards were able by these and other methods to
make fair-sized catches among the Theosophists, but it
was hard to hold some of these disciples of the out-spoken
Blavatsky, who warned her students of astral "spooks."
Many got into the movement, but got out when the
"blasting" with the "Blue Lightning" threatened too much
carnage in the land.

Fair hauls were also made from members of the various
Rosicrucian societies in America. But, like the Theosophists, those who did not get rid of their intellects, got out;
those who did, no doubt are still there.

From the Spiritualists, or those inclined that way, the Ballards naturally made many converts. Which is very understandable, considering that the Ballard cult itself is nothing but a glorified spiritualism with streamlined additions.

And yet, of all people who have ever condemned spiritualism, the Ballards have been the worst! They practiced the very thing they condemned, but distorted it, adding so much which is illegitimate and absurd that it has been a real detriment to the scientific investigation of spiritualism. They unwisely opened the psychic plane to people who have no comprehension of or control over the forces they have been led to play with, interfering with their proper focus on the physical plane of being, and threatening their mental balance.

No doubt the Ballards have made their greatest catches among students who have been associated with one or more of the various metaphysical organizations scattered throughout the United States. Most of these schools had been teaching about the "I AM" long years before Mrs. Ballard set herself up as an authority on the I AM in all languages.

The Ballards have drawn many from the Unity School of Christianity at Kansas City, and the variously-named Divine Science, New Thought, and Spiritual Healing groups.

The bait the Ballards used in getting converts from the various metaphysical schools was usually a more dynamic presentation of the "I AM," the greater lure of material prosperity, health, and the addition of streamlined "Masters" and "Goddesses." With so potent a combination, is it any wonder so many of the ever-growing numbers of metaphysically-inclined people in America fell for the Great Deception?

The Ballards have been particularly desirous, it seems, of getting the disciples of Mary Baker Eddy into their fold; and in their efforts to do this, have gone to extremes of both denunciation and flattery.

Thinking, perhaps, that the Christian Scientists would be more responsive to a feminine personality than a masculine one, they brought forth one of the "lady Ascended Masters," whom they called the *"Lady Master Leto."*

Leto "came forth" at the Pasadena, California, class, on the evening of January 17, 1937, and among other things she quite generously admitted that *"Mrs. Eddy brought another phase of Knowledge to Mankind."* Then in the usual Ballard way, loyal Leto, who, like other Ballard "Goddesses," has a good sense of advertising values, referred to the *"Saint Germain I AM Instruction,"* and said: "Now, *this* has come forth as the *final Knowledge"!* (p. 226, A. M. L.)

But the outspoken "Saint Germain," not so lady-like and diplomatic as little Leto, threatens to *"empty their churches"* if the Christian Scientists do not allegedly stop criticizing the Mighty I AM. We quote:

" . . . I tell you frankly, EVERY SOURCE, whether it is Unity, Christian Science or whatever it is that attempts to bring disgrace upon This Work or condemns or criticises It will fail utterly and their churches will be empty!" (p. 10, March, 1937, v.)

For the most part, we think Saint Germain waxes a little over-enthusiastic about the emptying of the Christian Science churches, and the others.

Doubtless some of the more restless souls of the Mother Church have become loosened from the C. S. imperturbable rock of faith and have fallen into Ballardism—Saint Germain's *"final knowledge"* of Christian Science!

And some of these have come out again—sadly disillusioned—and like wandering planetoids with irregular orbits are seeking some parent sun in the religious cosmos, some focus of more dependable faith than Ballardism with its strange coterie of man-made gods and goddesses.

CHAPTER 28

THE COURSE OF POLITICAL DICTATORSHIPS

The Ballard cult is but one of the increasing number of subversive influences in America today seeking, under various cloaks, to bring widespread confusion in the land.

Tyrannies of this kind do not wear labels on their coat sleeves telling the world what they intend to do. They work insidiously, under false fronts and colors, and only perhaps when they have achieved some degree of influence and power will their subversive nature be revealed.

When hundreds of thousands of adult Americans can embrace the Ballard doctrines without investigation, and accept ridiculous and unsupported statements on the word of two individuals, does it not indicate that some peculiar psychological influence is at work? Does it not suggest that something is happening to the American people, something is breaking down their reason and common sense, when movements such as Ballardism can make headway in our country?

Should this happen to any great extent, then political tyrannies can make inroads into our government and make this country something far different than contemplated by the signers of the Declaration of Independence and the framers of our American Constitution.

Then, when people awake to the menace, it may be too late to win back the liberties they have lost.

By that time, a dictatorship has been set up, with a controlled press, a regimented army and police force; and until that dictatorship has run its course, little can be done toward a new birth of freedom.

The Mighty I AM movement is an abortive effort to

make the American people into automatons, fitted only to obey the mandates of some dictator. The method of doing this has been the time-tested one of cloaking subversive doctrines in patriotic and religious observances.

"Save America! Support the Constitution! Adore your Mighty I AM!"

They organize "Minute Men" and "Daughters of Light"; have them meet in sacred "I AM Temples," wave the flag, sing stirring patriotic songs, and shout paeans of praise to unseen "Masters," who dictate the course of their lives.

Although their followers may be sincere in doing these things, nevertheless, it is very evident—when one gets behind the movement and sees the demands for obedience by two physical-plane dictators—that such religious and patriotic observances are but smoke screens.

When these cult leaders blaspheme Christ by bringing forth an astral "spook" on the stage and force their people through fear and intimidation to obey the mandates of some supposedly all-powerful "God" or "Goddess," is this real religion?

When they decree that an "Ascended Master" or some "Friend" be placed in every important political seat of the Government, and cajole their students into being absolutely subservient to the dictates of these so-called "Masters" and their earth-plane agents, is this by any chance the kind of patriotism embodied in our American Constitution and its Bill of Rights?

How absurd it is for these people to play up the Constitution and shout decrees to support it, when they are doing everything in their power to break it down!

How hypocritical it is for them to shout decrees to the "Blessed Master Jesus," when they teach idolatrous and paranoiac doctrines, breaking down the very ideals of humility, kindness, and service which the Master of Galilee came to teach!

How dangerous to the sanity of their people it is for them to launch upon the world an avalanche of monstrous fear-concepts—black magicians, cataclysms, astral entities, death rays, and other hobgoblins of the mind!

All this is part of a plan for world confusion, organized certainly by the Satanic powers of this universe, to which the Ballards, perhaps unconsciously, are giving expression —a plan designed to kill out individualism, our ideals of religious and political freedom, and eventually set up a dictatorship in liberty-loving America.

The preparation for a dictatorship begins years in advance. The course of it is slow and insidious, during which the minds of the people are lulled into byways and highways. Then, suddenly, one day, it is upon them, almost out of the blue; and it is then too late to take concerted action against it. The dictator is safely entrenched in the seat of power, with money and an army to enforce his mandates.

In Europe and Asia, dictatorships flourish by reason of might of arms and fears of the prison camps.

In America, if a dictatorship is to develop, it must first be psychological rather than physical.

Before actual, political dictatorship can arise in a republic, the minds of the people must be prepared and molded by propaganda of many kinds.

Anything which tends to keep people in an apathetic frame of mind, away from contact with reality, easily lends itself to some future political dictatorship.

For this reason, various peace proposals, non-resistance programs, metaphysical and religious teachings *may* peculiarly become good soils for the growth of some future dictatorship.

This is not said, of course, to reflect on any sincere effort toward peace or to discourage any true religious worship. But in so far as these matters may come under control of selfish individuals or misguided ones, there is naturally some danger that the unthinking mass of follow-ers may be led into programs which make for slavery in-stead of freedom.

The Ballard cult is one of those psychological influ-ences in America which is drawing, or attempting to draw, people's attention away from fundamentals; and by use of what virtually amounts to hypnotic control over their followers is preventing them from looking sanely at the problems which confront our Nation.

Expecting their individual and national salvation to come as a miraculous visitation from heaven in the form of some mighty "Master" who will straighten out their problems if they decree loud enough, the Ballard I AM-ers are lying supinely on their backs blissfully awaiting the inevitable disaster which would result if all of us turned our independence over to fake "psychic Masters" and scheming human beings.

To prevent such a dictatorship from arising in Amer-ica, either from the present Ballard cult or some other set-up, we need to be awake and alert as to what is going on. We must be keenly aware of the insidious, under-cover methods of those who would enslave us.

We cannot afford to "take our minds off every political and national affair," as the astral "Saint Germain" has urged his students to do.

We must not let this insidious thing which is attempt-ing to sweep in from Europe, Asia, and from the psychical-ly-disturbed world around us disarm our independence.

We must beware of movements and cults which out-wardly come in sheep's clothing of goodness, but inwardly are as ravenous as wolves.

We must not let the world confusion break down our faith in God, or in our own inherent, divinely-given wis-dom to work out of any disorder which may now or later confront us.

We must realize that America's problems are our own;

and we cannot leave them for God to solve for us, any more than a school child can be permitted to turn his lessons over to his father or teacher for solution.

Nor should we ever let any so-called "Master"—ascended or un-ascended—rule our lives for us; for no real Master of the Divine Wisdom would ever interfere with a pupil's God-given right of independent and initiative action.

For all these rights of independence and freedom the early pioneers of this Nation fought. They revolted against political and religious tyranny, which resulted in a Declaration of Rights which gave the American people the greatest amount of freedom and independence of any nation on earth.

Let us, therefore, be jealous of any and all these rights and privileges which we so far have held on to, and not permit the heel of any dictator within or without our borders, physical or psychic, to crush out this spirit of independence in freedom-loving America.

CHAPTER 29

"PEEWEE HITLERISM" IN AMERICA

In the summer of 1939 the House Committee to Investigate Un-American Activities, under the chairmanship of Martin Dies of Texas, made its report concerning some of the so-called patriotic movements in America.

The committee in that report concluded that many of these so-called patriotic movements "ape the methods of foreign dictators." These "peewee Hitlers," it said, are engaged in "a form of racketeering" and in "subversive activities," and are trying to bring about "a radical change in the American form of government."

It called special attention "to the deplorable prostitution of such words as 'patriotism' and 'Christian' to the selfish ends of these fascist racketeers."

As all of this has a bearing upon the movement which we are exposing, it is well to take a short retrospect of the astonishing number of political and so-called patriotic movements which have arisen in our country during the last several years.

Most of these movements are generally considered to be American fascist organizations. They are built usually on the personal leadership of a single individual whose spleen is directed against either real or imaginary evils within the government. Their avowed purpose is to save the people from certain "enemies" which assertedly seek to overthrow the democracy and establish some other form of government in its place. In "saving" the country, these organizations usually seek to bring about a new government of their own!

Among some of the outstanding "American fascist" groups is William Dudley Pelley's "Silver Shirt Legion." Elsewhere we have referred to the similarity between the Pelley and Ballard movements. It was brought out that Pelley started out originally as a psychic or metaphysical leader, and then rapidly arose to become a political fuehrer with "storm troopers" or legionnaires in every state.

The Ballards likewise are psychic leaders, but have political ambitions too. Their "Master" in the early days, as we have seen, sought to take over the Pelley movement. They have since organized Minute Men, or, as we might say, "storm troopers" in every state.

The Silver Shirt leader has evidently over-reached himself in his ambitions to become the "American Hitler," the fuehrer of the United States. He has been accused by the Dies Committee of printing and distributing literature "containing scurrilous, false and perfidious assertions, and reprints of propaganda of a foreign power," according to a brief filed in the District Court in Washington by counsel for the Dies Committee.

For a number of weeks Pelley was a fugitive from the Dies Committee which wanted to serve him with a subpoena and question him concerning his activities. He later, however, showed up before this committee, admitted "a change of heart," and showered glowing adjectives of approval upon the committee's work. Convicted in 1935 for violating the North Carolina "blue sky" securities law, his sentence was suspended, but it appears that he is now wanted by North Carolina authorities for violating the conditions of his parole.

The record of the Ballard printings and assertions is likewise notorious, and as we have already seen, Ballard too has had difficulties with the "blue sky" securities law. The amazing thing is that this evident subversive movement should have continued so long without an investigation by this same Dies committee which went after Pelley and some of the other fascist movements so strongly. No doubt its "religious" set-up protects it.

Racketeers who hide under the cloak of religion are likely to become one of the most dangerous and difficult problems in the future, if not, indeed, at the present time. It is the weak spot in our protective armor against "Fifth Columns"; and although the main approach to it must be, as always, through education and enlightenment of the people and the public exposure of the methods of the religious charlatan, still, there is a real need for more courageous action by our public officials who should not swerve aside merely because a dangerous and subversive movement operates as a "religion."

There are said to be at least a hundred American fascist organizations which have attracted the attention of the Dies Committee, whose records have been or are being investigated.

The subpoenaing of Maj. Gen. George Van Horn Moseley in May, 1939, to testify about his story concerning an alleged Jewish plot to seize America gave wide publicity to these fascist organizations, revealing to the public how prevalent today is this battle of individuals and their organizations against real or fancied evil which threaten our country.

It brought up for investigation the various anti-Semitic movements, some of which the Dies Committee characterized as "a most violent type."

The Knights of the White Camellia, headed by George E. Deatherage; the Crusading White Shirts of George W. Christians; and other movements of similar nature, dominated usually by some racial or religious intolerance, are in active operation in the United States today.

The present political power of the Detroit radio priest, Father Coughlin, shows to what extent the personality of one man can sway the thoughts and actions of millions.

The danger in all such movements lies in inflaming the

minds of irresponsible and misguided individuals, leading to street fights, mob uprisings, and the use of arms to put down "other uprisings." Whenever this philosophy of hatred is preached, the spirit of the mob may readily be aroused, and the movement may get out of control of the one who originated it.

Among the Coughlinites, as among the Ballardites, have appeared so-called "*Minute Men*," differently organized and controlled, but bearing the same name.

Gerald Winrod's Defenders of the Christian Faith is another of the American fascist groups whose influence has been wide-spread among certain orthodox religious bodies who, like the Pelleyites and Coughlinites, profess to see the menace of Jewry in America.

The German American Bund, outpost for Hitler's Western Hemisphere ambitions, has for years been insidiously spreading the philosophy of Nazism throughout the United States. Some of these American fascist movements formerly paid open allegiance to Hitler's ideology, and it was not until the German fuehrer's astonishing tie-up with Communist Russia and the imprisonment in America of the bundfuehrer, Fritz Kuhn, on a misappropriation of funds conviction that some of these fascist leaders in America half-heartedly withdrew their allegiance to Hitler. Perhaps Hitler's blitzkrieg on Europe has completed their disillusionment.

All of these American fascist movements are reciprocal, i.e., one builds on the work of the other. Yet, the desire for personal power and many individual rivalries makes them incapable of raising a single leader who can represent and control them all. That is the weakness of the American fascist movement today, which is fortunate for our present constituted government.

Arrayed against these heterodox fascist groups are the organized left-wing radical groups themselves—the Communists and their offshoots. They seek to change the

American form of government by injecting ideologies of their own, even going so far as to openly preach the gospel of revolution to bring in the new government.

And in this latest and weirdest organization of them all, known as the "Mighty I AM," directed by its two fuehrers with the aid of so-called "Ascended Masters," there is represented a most amazing conglomeration of forces and ideologies, largely psychic or psychological in character, which is being thrown against a medley of "evils" of various kinds and which is undoubtedly producing many evils of its own.

Surely, if ever a country was besieged by an army of embattled "shirts" of various stripes and colors, it is our country today!

A fervid patriotism is usually the explosive spark which propels these movements on their careers. They receive their power through "hating" something, and, conversely, through "loving" something. Without this emotional combustion there would be no force to propel them against the objects of their dislikes.

And always, whether they fight for a democracy, a communistic state, or an imperialistic autocracy, they must proceed through the power of a *dictator*.

To bring in their ideal of a "democracy," they, oddly enough, start a little *dictatorship!* Something in itself the exact reverse of a true democracy.

Or else, like the American Nazis, they openly espouse an out-and-out dictatorship and hold up the ideal of a foreign government and its fuehrer.

It is this tendency toward a dictatorship which, despite their differing ideologies, makes all these movements brothers under the skin. They *all* seek to bring about some kind of dictatorship in America.

The Bund fuehrer wants to impose Nazism, the Communist works for his so-called dictatorship by the proletariat, the Ku-Klux-Klaner wants a little private dictatorship of his own, and some of the American fascist groups hint at a military dictatorship.

At the Moseley and Deatherage hearings before the Dies Committee it was asserted that *"military action would be necessary to get the gang out,"* referring to an alleged Jewish plot to overthrow the American form of government. The fascist remedy, as brought out in the Dies hearings, is for a *"military court"* to take control of the Federal government and each of the 48 states.

Such fascist movements are usually counter-revolutionary—organizations set up to check alleged revolutionary movements which they consider the government unable to cope with, or may even be a party to, and so they seek to bring about a little revolution of their own and take over the reins of government themselves.

Doubtless some of the American fascist movements were originally founded on sincere patriotic ideals, but the evolution of them along emotional lines, with hate as their keynote, inevitably brings about the rise of mob psychology, the oppression of a minority, and a tyrannical dictatorship.

And now in this latest fascist-directed movement, popularly known as the Mighty I AM, we see many similarities to the methods of these other movements—yet, it is the strangest dictatorship of them all.

It is a "PSYCHIC DICTATORSHIP," and it functions by means of the purported power and authority of a score or more of unseen "Ascended Masters," who have for five years used as their mouthpieces two earth-plane fuehrers!

It is effective to the extent that people love, fear, or believe one Guy Ballard and his wife Edna, the emissaries of the psychic Dictator, "Saint Germain," who told his "beloved family" that they will have a part to play in bringing into perfection "that Government of so long ago into America at this time," and that the "New Government will require their services ere long."

Now, in this cult's attempt to set up an alien dictatorship of "Ascended Masters," with the two fuehrers as
representatives, there is revealed much of the same paran-
oid tendencies and delusions of grandeur which we find so
manifest in the Hitlerian ideology.

One cannot read Adolf Hitler's *Mein Kampf* without
recognizing in Ballardism a great deal of the same cunning
strategy, the same psychology, which brought the German
fuehrer into power.

Patriotism, hate, and the lie have been the subtle psychological weapons of this foreign despot, whose methods
are being duplicated today, or drawn from the same hidden
invisible source, by the Saint Germain cult.

Referring to his gospel of *hate,* Hitler says: "For pure-
ly psychological reasons one must present not two enemies
to the masses, but only one! A single enemy must be pushed
forward and all hate must be concentrated upon this sole
opponent."

This "master psychologist" goes on to say: "It is part
of the genius of a true leader to make even widely different enemies appear to belong to but a single category
. . . " And then this fuehrer of the German peoples lumps
all his hatreds together—and calls them Jews!

The Ballard hatreds are likewise legion, ranging all the
way from allergic Ascended Masters' hatred of garlic and
onions to violent tirades against "black magicians," "communists," "spies," and "vicious individuals" who oppose
their work. And, like Hitler, they lump all their hatreds
under a single category—and call it the "Sinister Force"!

Having propounded in his book his doctrine of a single
hate, Dictator Hitler goes on to stress the psychological
value of the *enormous lie.*

"The primitive simplicity of the mind of the masses,"
he says, "is more easily misled by a great than a tiny lie."

He goes on to say the masses are "accustomed to telling

insignificant lies," and can therefore "detect such lies in others."

"But," says this master strategist, "they generally fail to detect a truly gigantic distortion!"

In a similar way the Ballards have either consciously or unconsciously followed the Hitler strategy. Can one think of any more "enormous lie," any more truly "gigantic distortion," than that represented in the Ballard cult?

If ever "peewee Hitlerism" in America becomes more like its big brother abroad, it will be because the American people fail to realize, and take steps to counteract, the subtle psychic or psychological inroads that are being made by various movements in this country.

CHAPTER 30

THE BALLARD "INNER SECRET SERVICE"

There is reason to wonder whether the United States Government, and especially J. Edgar Hoover's F.B.I., is aware that operating in our country alongside of the government's own Secret Service is another "Secret Service" operated by the "Ascended Masters" of the Ballard cult!

Surprising as this may seem to the Federal Bureau of Investigation and to others, we are assured by the Ballards themselves that such is unquestionably the case.

We quote directly from the stenographic record of the Chief of the Ballard "Inner Secret Service," whose secret code name is K-17. This great investigator for the "Ascended Masters" came forth on the stage of the Shrine Civic Auditorium at Los Angeles on January 1, 1939 (at least Guy Ballard said he did), and publicly revealed some of the inner secrets of his secret service work and its connection with J. Edgar Hoover's F.B.I.

"Beloved ones," said the I.S.S. Chief, "there has been throughout the centuries an Inner Secret Service in connection with certain ones of the outer Secret Service. You will notice that I am not hesitating to give this information. It will be well for all individuals to listen to that! America is going to have her protection! (applause)

" . . . The greater part of my twenty-four hours are spent in the tangible body in the outer world! Therefore, there is nothing can be hidden from me (applause) and when I start out to get evidence I get it! (applause) . . .

"You have many Friends in the outer Secret Service

as well as the Inner; (applause) . . . "(p. 13, Feb., 1939, v.)

Long before the new I.S.S. Chief came on the job, Guy Ballard in his books told of his secret service connections. While assertedly living at the Rayborn "Diamond K Ranch" in Wyoming in the fall of 1931, a secret agent by name of Gaylord arrived, presented his credentials and told of his "personal contact with some of the higher official and diplomatic circles in Washington." (p. 166, M. P.)

"Saint Germain," continued this secret agent, "is concerned with certain activities in Washington at the present time It is his request that we three reach there the second of October, and he will meet us on our arrival. He says it is possible to use you in certain ways . . . Remember always, that our eternal motto and rule of conduct is—'To know, to dare, to do, and to be silent.' "

Then Ballard—daring but not so *silent*—goes on to tell further details about his secret service experiences. He, Rayborn, and the secret agent start on their journey to official Washington, during which journey they receive important information concerning "two of the communist representatives," one of them, a woman, admittedly "one of the cleverest, most dangerous, and notorious persons in Europe." (p. 178, M. P.)

"Put on your armor," said Gaylord to Ballard, "for in handling this woman, when the time comes, you will need to use all your powers of diplomacy. You have a part to fulfill more important than you dream . . . We are getting into action here none too soon."

On this dangerous and "secret" mission, Ballard, entertained by many a thrilling secret-service story from Gaylord, eventually arrives in Washington—the Washington that was *his*, for was he not the reincarnated George Washington, the first President of the United States? What memories this visit must have brought back!

However, in his absorption he forgets completely to follow up his story of the interesting woman who was "one of the cleverest, most dangerous, and notorious persons in Europe." Whether his "diplomatic powers" were equal to the task of handling this woman we shall unfortunately perhaps never know. But let him continue with his other exploits.

"The third day after our arrival," writes Ballard, "Rayborn, Gaylord, and I, accompanied by Saint Germain and certain members of the Secret Service, went to the rendezvous of an important group of those who were willing channels for the sinister force. There were present the seven principal leaders in America.

" . . . We walked in upon them, Saint Germain charging the atmosphere with an electric force that held them immovable. Their drawn guns dropped to the floor where they stood, and their arms hung motionless by their sides. . .

"The members of the Secret Service stepped forward, and took them into custody, where they shall remain until they serve 'THE LIGHT.' " (pp. 212-213, M. P.)

But K-17's "Inner Secret Service" does not always, it seems, work in such perfect conjunction with J. Edgar Hoover's outer F.B.I. Sometimes the I.S.S. takes things in its own hands, evidently not willing to wait on the slower-moving but perhaps more thorough-going F.B.I.

As a case in point, we cite the achievement of Saint Germain who by himself, without any assistance from the outer Secret Service whatsoever, discovered a diabolical foreign plot against the United States. It was at San Francisco on February 5, 1938, that he revealed the astonishing service which he performed for his adopted country.

"A concentrated action," he said, "was attempted in the Orient and in Europe to band together certain aerial forces to bring destruction to our America. Five times, I intercepted their messengers. In the case of the last one, I was compelled to turn back upon him his own viciousness, which destroyed his physical body."

Then the thoroughly aroused Saint Germain sent back a message to the originators of this attack, saying:

"If you attempt further destructive activity of that kind, and you start those planes for America, I will destroy every one and the people that are in them! . . . If necessary, I will destroy your whole army! and if you think I cannot do it, try it out!" (p. 3, March, 1938, v.)

That was certainly definite enough for any foreign foe to our American freedom, or any combination of powers. But it seems they took Saint Germain's warning too lightly. They did not start *planes* for America, but did send three *submarines!*

And now we must let the Chief of the I.S.S. himself tell what happened to them, because, for some reason, "Saint Germain" was not in on the destruction that follows.

It was in Chicago on the afternoon of September 3, 1939, that this I.S.S. Chief known as K-17 suddenly appeared on the stage of the Civic Opera House. Although K-17 claims that most of the time he is in his "tangible body," it appears that no one else saw or heard him except Guy Ballard, so we shall have to take his word for it.

"Beloved Children of the Light," said Chief K-17, "I come on a very urgent mission today. Three submarines are on their way to the Panama Canal. I ask you to make the call and I guarantee you that within the hour, they will not exist. (applause)"

So for one hour and twenty-five minutes the I AM-ers assembled at the big opera house in Chicago decreed and decreed, and sang a song or two, and all the while down at Panama things were happening. Then at exactly 4:10 P. M. (25 minutes late), K-17 returned to make his report:

"Beloved Children of the Light," he announced, "you have gratitude to Us—We have gratitude to you for supplying that which We required in giving forth this Service to mankind.

"Three of the remaining five secret submarines are no more! (applause)

"One was within sixty miles of the Panama Canal, so We had to act very quickly . . .

"This plan to destroy the Panama Canal has been long and well laid. They did not consider Us, but We were Real enough to destroy those destructive ships and the people in them. (applause) . . .

"Long ago in the coming forth of the books you were informed that there was the Inner Secret Service, in many ways more powerful than the outer secret service. When the Inner Secret Service acts, as a rule the individuals disappear from the earth.

"I will not tell you in just what time or how long it took to consume them, but not long. Three hundred and sixty-four foreign spies will act no more in your beloved America! (applause)" (pp. 30-31, Oct., 1939, v.)

So far as we have been able to discover, no acknowledgment or thanks have been extended by the F.B.I. or the War Department for the meritorious services of the I.S.S. and the "I AM" for saving the Panama Canal.

We feel that the matter should most definitely be looked into by the Federal Government and proper steps taken to reward the parties concerned.

CHAPTER 31

DECREES OF DEATH!

The Ballards have not only by fear and threat and by flattery and cajolery tried to keep their movement from disintegrating, but they have in their decrees against individuals called upon the Mighty Powers of Heaven to destroy *physically* those who sought in any way to interfere with it.

It seems a strange and fantastic thing, but for over five years large groups of people throughout the United States have been meeting together and shouting decrees which have for their purpose the *"dissolving," "consuming," "annihilating," "blasting," "exploding,"* and *"destroying"* of certain human beings, or the political or religious organizations which they represent.

They project at their meetings what they call the destructive "BLUE LIGHTNING," analogous it seems to the "DEATH RAY" of the pulp magazines, and if the reader should happen to pass an I AM Temple or "Sanctuary," he would be very likely to hear reverberating out upon the street the loud shouting of the following decree:

"*STOP! STOP! STOP!* YOU HAVE NO POWER! YOUR DAY IS DONE! BE THOU DISSOLVED AND CONSUMED BY THE POWER OF LIGHT!"

In an effort to show the power of these "Blue-Lightning" blasts, Guy Ballard at the Chicago class on May 8, 1938, said:

"You five hundred thousand students have been calling into action the Power of the Blue Lightning! Do you know what that means? Do you know one day the momentum gained in that action, if necessary, will be released! and no matter how terrifying It is to humanity, *That Power Shall Be Released!*" ("Goddess of Liberty" dictation, page 2, May 19, 1938, Group Letter.)

In the Ballard "*I AM Decree Book*," copyrighted by the Saint Germain Press, there are seventy-one decrees intended to meet all their needs, from controlling the state of the weather to the state of the nation! The book presents a curious litany of hate, love, and intolerant rule over the life and liberties of others.

The following are parts of some of the other decrees which are shouted from coast to coast:

"*SILENCE* the tongue and make *HELPLESS* and inactive all attempts to interfere with or cast discredit upon this I AM Instruction! . . . *BLAST* and *ANNIHILATE* all that would interfere in any way with this Perfection! . . . Project the Blue Lightning into every one of these vortices of human discord . . . and *EXPLODE, EXPLODE, EXPLODE* every one this instant!"

On the evening of October 21, 1937, in New York City, Guy Ballard shouted to his audience the following decree:

"I call the Angels of Blue Lightning, the Legions of Light to stand guard over your America; My America; that every person who tries to bring destructive conditions, qualities or activities into America, SHALL CEASE TO EXIST IN HIS HUMAN FORM!" (p. 23, Dec., 1937, v., our capitals.)

The above is a decree for *death!* It takes one back in imagination to some aboriginal jungle where some native medicine man with savage incantations and rites is decreeing the death of his enemy. Books dealing with witchcraft, sorcery, and demonology are full of this sort of thing, but we hardly expect it in civilized America. Yet this decree for the destruction of a human form was publicly uttered on the stage of the Engineering Auditorium in our own New York City!

If it be thought this death decree was merely a slip of the tongue made in the excitement of the moment, the reader should be disillusioned. Such a thing is a studied and regular activity of this black-magic organization.

In making these death decrees Ballard sometimes tries to hide behind what he calls his own "Mighty I AM Presence," and says that it is his "I AM" speaking and not Ballard. If so, Ballard's "I AM" is a dangerous and death-dealing "I AM," and most sensible people would have nothing whatever to do with it.

Speaking at West Palm Beach, Florida, on the afternoon of December 5, 1937, Guy Ballard stated:

"Ere long the light shall compel every human being, every human form, to give the necessary obedience to Me, the Mighty I AM . . . When It reaches a certain state of vibratory action, the human form who will not give obedience becomes DISSOLVED." (p. 12, Jan, 1938, v., our capitals.)

At Cleveland on the afternoon of November 14, 1936, "Mighty I AM" Ballard shouted:

"I AM the Presence that silences and *places out of action* every person, association or whatever sends forth destructive activity to My Presentation . . . of this Light and work! . . . All unfortunate individuals in human form who henceforth attempt to personally interfere with this Light . . . SHALL MEET the recoil of their own destructive creation . . . There is no Power in heaven or earth to stop it . . . I HAVE SPOKEN!" (pp. 3 and 9, Jan., 1937, v., their capitals.)

Most often, however, instead of hiding behind his "I AM," Ballard takes cover behind some supposedly great "Ascended Master," and has this great Being say and do things of which not even the most ordinary of human beings would be guilty—and certainly not a real Master of Wisdom.

It is easy to discover that the Ballard "Gods" and "Goddesses" are all created in the image of their maker. We find them without exception expressing the thoughts, feelings, and grammatical errors of their creators.

Once when Edna Ballard was reading one of Saint Germain's (?) discourses, a former school girl friend dryly remarked: "Edna, you should not have Saint Germain make the same grammatical errors that you made in class."

It is not to be wondered at, therefore, that the Ballard "lady and gentlemen Ascended Masters" are just as proficient in throwing the "Blue Lightning" as are the Ballards. The following threats of death are all taken from the Ballard literature, and supposedly made by great "Ascended Masters."

"Those who try to oppose this Light are *dissolved* by it . . . Destructive individuals shall be searched out and *shall leave those bodies* . . . I would *dissolve those physical bodies* before they shall harm him . . . They sound their own *death knell!* . . . When It moves into action everything unlike Itself dissolves and disappears before It! If that *includes some of mankind's bodies,* then shall it be so!" Etc., etc.

Openly revealing a sadistic tendency, "Saint Germain," at the Minneapolis class threatened to draw these vicious individuals before him and "*see them cry out in agony.*" A little later, he boasted: "*We have our own means of causing people to disappear.*" (pp. 26-27, Oct., 1939, v.)

"Mighty Cosmo," another of the Ballard fraternity of avenging gods, said at Los Angeles: "The insane human beings that try to spread doubt concerning the Glory of these Messengers . . . *should be shut up forever* . . . no longer may mercy be shown to those who willfully turn away from this Light . . . better had a rattlesnake woven itself in among you than the poisonous breath of doubt. (applause) . . . If they do not stop it, they will *sting themselves to death!* (applause)" (pp. 8-12-16-18, Aug., 1939, v., our italics.)

Emphasizing this idea of destruction of the physical body, Ballard came out on the stage of the Shrine Auditorium in Los Angeles on Wednesday, July 6, 1938, and said that "Saint Germain" would have the dictation.

"I ask you," said Saint Germain, "to watch these unfortunate creatures who have tried to destroy the work of the Messengers and My Work. One of the worst ones in America is here in your city. Watch the reaction of their own DESTRUCTION. It must return upon themselves— it is the Law of Life, so the Law will take its toll. Therefore, I trust BY SUNDAY I shall have still *added joyful news for you*." (p. 17, Aug., 1938, v., our capitals and italics.)

Is it not evident from "Saint Germain's" remark of "added joyful news by Sunday," that he expected something *physically* to happen to a certain Los Angeles person within four days?

At the following Shrine Class in Los Angeles, held six months later, there seemed to have been much discouragement about the slowness of action of these *"Death Rays"* upon certain individuals. The Ballards therefore gave their chief G-man, K-17 of the "Inner Secret Service," additional work to do—and the Chief of the I.S.S. did not hesitate to say that *"physical action"* would be necessary. We quote:

"The Messenger said to you, I think it was on last Tuesday, that he felt the attempted opposition to this Great Light had been dissolved. It has on the Inner action of life but there are still things to be done in the outer . . .

"Beloved students in the future, *do not hesitate to put down anything* that tries to defame This Work. You have My permission! (applause) . . .

"Your Mighty Decrees have been answered remarkably so far and they will be answered in a more and more remarkable way; but, since time is an essential in this, *We shall take a part in PHYSICAL ACTION.*

"... The unfortunate individuals who ... have tried in every conceivable way to bring disgrace upon This Work, watch that disgrace return upon them! (applause) DO NOT HESITATE TO HELP IT ALONG, beloved students. (applause)" (pp. 12-13, Feb., 1939, v., our capitals and italics.)

It is evident from the above that the Ballard decrees for destruction do not work, and that, therefore, this "Secret Service Master," who says he has a "tangible body," is going to take a part in some "PHYSICAL ACTION." Whatever it is that he has in mind, the Ballard students are urged to "*help it along*" and to "*put down anything*" which works against their movement. And the audience, emotionally aroused with the spirit of the mob, applauds and applauds.

If it was the intention of this "Secret Service Master" to arouse members in the audience to take some kind of "physical action" against individuals who were revealing certain facts about this cult, then it was not altogether unsuccessful.

At least in the case of the writer it was so, for on the evening of January 13th—twelve days after K-17's "permission" to students to "put down anything that tries to defame This Work"—he was decoyed to a dead-end street in Los Angeles, where several members of a gang were waiting to do him bodily harm. He recognized in time, however, that it was a hold up, and was able to get away without being injured; but for a number of days following this experience he received telephone calls from various members of the gang threatening him bodily harm if he didn't "lay off" the Mighty I AM.

This thing of inflaming the mind to destructive action against so-called "vicious individuals" is one of the most dangerous aspects of this cult. Imagine the possible effect on certain types of emotional, unbalanced individuals when statements like the following are made. They were made publicly in Philadelphia on November 15, 1938, by Guy Ballard, but if you can believe it—they are the actual words of the *Archangel Michael!*

"Since more than six hundred thousand people are calling for Me . . . they shall wield the Sword of Blue Flame in their PHYSICAL HANDS. (p. 7, Jan., 1939, v.)

"Therefore, tonight, I release to you in Philadelphia the Power of the use of the Sword of Blue Flame. Mentally, picture it in your hands. (pp. 8-9.)

"These forces that hate so greatly and do all they can to spread discord everywhere, must be governed; sometimes by FORCE! That is what We shall proceed to do . . . Therefore, when We tell you that We intend to use FORCE where it is necessary, We mean just that! We mean the force and Power of Light that can absolutely SILENCE ANY HUMAN ACTION! . . . That is why there will be thousands of students in America in the near future who can say *"STOP!"* with a force that will FASTEN THE HUMAN FORM IN ITS TRACKS." (pp. 12-13, our capitals.)

Imagine making such dangerous promises and placing in the hands of emotionally-aroused people such imaginary power!

In any large meeting of this kind there are likely to be present those who are mentally unbalanced, psychopathic, or perhaps criminally insane. Fired with the ardor of being able to wield Archangel Michael's "Sword of Blue Flame" in their "physical hands," there is no telling what such individuals might do physically against any so-called vicious person; for when their decrees of death do not work on the mental plane of being, the tendency is to go over to the physical.

When such a mob spirit as this gets loose in America under the guise of religion and patriotism, does it not constitute a danger and a menace?

CHAPTER 32

THE "BLUE LIGHTNING" FLASHES AT CLEVELAND

We shall now recount stirring events which led up to the inauguration of a new system of attendance at the Ballard classes.

For five years the "Accredited Messengers of Saint Germain" had *openly* preached their political ond religious doctrines to the American people.

Suddenly, however, following a hectic 10-day class at Cleveland in October, 1939, all this was changed.

Then began their new system of holding all meetings "*closed*," open only to those who would sign pledges of allegiance to the "Ascended Masters" and their three-and-only Accredited Messengers.

One of the reasons for this change from open to closed meetings was due, no doubt, to the fact that their meetings were getting a bit too fanatical and funny for the general public to tolerate.

The furious decreeing and condemnation of "spies" and other "enemies" from the platform, the lack of tolerance and true devotion, did not make the average unhexed newcomer feel that these people were altogether sane or inspired by a preponderance of Christian love and charity. They would perhaps notice the ungrammatical language used by "Perfect Beings from the Seventh Octave of Light," or they might even notice Guy Ballard taking his watch out to see how much time an all-knowing "Master" or "Goddess" had for the dictation—all of which would give rise to the unkind thought that it was only Guy Ballard himself dictating his own messages.

Such "vicious" individuals from the unregenerate public had to be dealt with in some way. They usually had
watchful Minute Men eject them from the auditorium,
but, as we shall see, some of these "storm troopers" of the
Ballards took their jobs a little bit too seriously.

Occasionally, too, some woman would object to the
removing of her hat—a little observance absolutely necessary to enable the great Saint Germain to send "Light
Rays" into her brain. Whether she gave the great "Master"
permission to do this or not, it was to be done unto her.
She, and everyone else, was drafted for complete "Light
Ray" service during the entire meeting. Bald-headed men,
it would appear, would have no protection at all from
Saint Germain's Light Ray.

Conscientious objectors to this rigid, hat-removing requirement of the Ascended Masters would be uncere-
moniously and, if necessary, forcefully ejected—the most
conscientious of them, all the while, voicing down the aisle
an audible protest.

A woman who had this experience happen to her in
Detroit, wrote to the writer as follows:

"I went to hear them yesterday and simply refused to
remove my hat or applaud them because I did not know
anything about their doctrines. I was ushered out because
of it . . . stopped the show for a while. If that 'Tube of
Light' of Saint Germain's could not penetrate a little bit
of cloth on my head, the 'God' they worship must be a
weak God."

Such happenings, of course, worked against the peace
and harmony of each miracle-working class; and, as we
shall see, sometimes brought about legal actions which the
bolt-throwing Thors of this cult could not handle with
their death-dealing "Blue Lightning."

Occasional disturbances of this kind were bad enough,
but when the Accredited Messengers reached Cleveland in
October, 1939, for the usual 10-day open meeting, it

seemed as if all the "sinister forces" of the universe had arrayed themselves against their "Powers of Light."

Part of the trouble that ensued was brought about by the Minute Men at the door being caught a little off guard, in that they permitted a bad-acting newspaper man by name of Westbrook Pegler, who possesses a particularly trenchant pen, to get into their meeting.

It further appears that neither G-man "Saint Germain" nor the great "Inner Secret Service" Chief himself, "K-17," knew that this nationally-known columnist was in the audience, or they would surely have sent their annihilating "Blue Lightning" at him, and that would have been the end of the matter!

Perhaps, too intent on directing their "Blue Lightning" at the enemy abroad, they neglected the nearer menace at their own door. At any rate, there he was—a sort of literary bull in an "Ascended-Master" china shop!

Now, as the trenchant-pen Pegler sat in meeting, pretty soon he was rubbing his eyes and doubting his ears. So many things were happening . . . foreign submarines being destroyed by Swords of Blue Flame . . . Japanese bombers being routed by Ascended Masters . . . William Shakespeare shaking his spear . . . etc. . . . etc. . . . that upon leaving, he said, he had to buy a "sheaf of books to confirm in print what he had heard in bewilderment from the platform."

So armed with the booklets, which doubtlessly assured him of his own sanity, and that *what* he had heard he had *really* heard and not imagined, he sat down and wrote the first of two articles on the strange cult, beginning in this wise:

"It seems impossible that in all history the human race has produced any more humiliating rebuke to its claims of reason and dignity than a certain congregation of about 1,000 Americans who have been gathering afternoons and evenings lately in Cleveland to take part in a religious cult known as the Great I AM."

He went on to say among other scathing denunciations in this first article, that it was "*the most revolting travesty in the entire record of religious eccentricity in the United States.*" (United Feature Syndicate, Oct. 24, 1939.)

This and his other article on the cult, appearing as they did in so many newspapers of a syndicated chain, brought much unfavorable publicity to the "Accredited Messengers" and their strange cult.

The "Blue Lightning" began to flash at this Cleveland class as never before, but too late now to stop the "sinister forces," other adverse things began to happen.

A Cleveland candid camera fan, while at the meeting attempted to photograph the camera-shy Accredited Messengers through a hole in his hat; but, as cameras are not permitted, he didn't quite get away with it.

One of the white-uniformed storm-troopers spied him in the act, and, according to the account in the Cleveland Press of October 25, "not only ripped the film from his camera but also knelt on his Adam's apple, bloodied his nose and removed small portions of epidermis from various parts of his face."

The result was a suit against the Accredited Messengers for $5,000, court attachments on 4 canary-yellow Chryslers, 1 "Ascended-Master" Harp, 1 earth-plane Novachord, and various and sundry stage props.

Following closely upon this was another suit for $5,000 made by a woman who refused to obey Saint Germain's mandate concerning the removal of hats. We quote an article in the *Cleveland Press* of October 25, 1939:

"Mrs. ——— asserts that she was forcibly ejected from the auditorium, suffering injuries to her spine, on Friday last, when she refused to remove her hat out of respect to the Great I AM. White clad ushers, or Minute Men, as they are known, flung her to the sidewalk, she asserts."

From these harrowing experiences at Cleveland and

with their "Blue Lightning" in full retreat, the Ballards moved on to the Eastern coast, temporarily minus their four canary-yellow cars, the "Ascended-Master" harp, and other necessities of their trade, which had been pasted all over with legal attachments at Cleveland—mere pieces of paper which Saint Germain's "Blue Lightning" could not dissolve quite so easily as it dissolved three considerably more weighty submarines just in time to save the Panama Canal.

Under such *un*-Ascended Master circumstances, the scheduled open meetings at Philadelphia and Washington were forthwith cancelled on order of "Saint Germain," and in those cities the new system of "closed" classes started.

Only the faithful and obedient students were gathered together at those classes; and the guards at the door, not depending so much on the stopping power of the "Blue Lightning," became *physically* more vigilant in their efforts to keep out process servers and bad-acting newspaper people.

On the afternoon of November 12, 1939, at Washington—*city of Guy Ballard's former victories as Commander-in-Chief of the Continental Army!*—the lovely "Goddess of Light" came forth to make a few pertinent remarks concerning recent happenings.

"These beloved Messengers," she said, "who have never harmed a fly have been set upon by such depraved creatures as put forth these articles. Those individuals will yet understand, they are dealing with a Power of Light with which they cannot cope." (p. 10, Feb., 1940, v.)

"Do not talk about these classes outside," continued the Goddess. "Spies are everywhere and in the future there will be no outer notice of when or where the classes are to be held . . . If spies and people come to you for information . . . tell them it is none of their business." (pp. 17-18.)

That same evening, "Saint Germain," more threatening in his remarks than the Goddess, told the class-leaders:

"You must take a more positive stand, release a force in those places and throw out people who get nosey. There is no law in this land that allows anybody to come into your place and snoop around." (p. 21, Feb., 1940, v.)

"You just wait, beloved ones, until these classes have been closed for six months or a year. If you do not see a scrambling in the outer world, then I will miss My guess." (p. 22.)

"We have a means recently established by which We can reach people, certain people at any time . . . This will help tremendously in the regulation of things and in the raising up of Ascended Master Friends . . . " (p. 25.)

" . . . The government has watched this Activity from the beginning and knows that there is not one harmful thing in it." (p. 25.)

"It is Our Intent and has been from the beginning that when We do begin to appear tangibly to you . . . to become a Law for the student body—and when We do that, I assure you there will be no Peglers or Millers. (applause)" [Miller is a newspaper man who exposed the cult in Cleveland.] (p. 31.)

Then dispatching a 400-word telegram to a Los Angeles class leader, firing him on the spot for disobedience, this now thoroughly-aroused "Ascended Master" said: "In the future all classes and groups will be closed to the outside world . . . Then the howling pack of wolves on the outside can howl to their hearts' content."

Having with proper threats inaugurated their "closed" classes in Washington and Philadelphia, the Ballards returned in the fall of 1939 to their great Mecca in Los Angeles.

At all former "Shrine" classes the "blessed people of Los Angeles" had always been lovingly invited—even though on their printed "invitation," they stated: "We always reserve the right to refuse admittance or have anyone removed from the audience at our discretion."

At this new "closed" class, however, only those of the "blessed public" who would *sign a pledge of allegiance to the Ballards and their "Ascended Masters"* could get in.

In addition, evidently afraid of further legal suits and acutely conscious of the failure of their "Blue Lightning" to handle such matters, they at this first "closed" Shrine class made the "blessed public" agree not to hold the Ballards responsible for anything that might happen at the classes.

So on both Eastern and Western Coasts there was started, at these closed classes, a new dispensation over the lives and liberties of their followers. No notes of any kind were permitted to be taken, and no information was to be given on the outside concerning this secret cult which today uses some of the methods of the German Gestapo. The statement was made that if anything leaks out, God help the one through whom it comes!

And as might be expected, these secret classes made the credulous members of the same blessed public even more anxious to be partakers in the "blessings" that were to be distributed in greater abundance than before, now that the "spies" and heretics were to be kept out.

There was a rush just before the start of the Shrine class on December 22, to fulfill "Ascended-Master" requirements of admission and to be the proud possessor of an "admission card" which would entitle the fortunate student to unobstructed entrance into these secret meetings.

And at this Shrine class, Edna Ballard, who already many times before had demonstrated her ability to surmount crises in the movement, was destined to rise to new heights and powers of her feminine dictatorship over her followers.

Six months before, in this city, when a minor crisis had arisen and certain staff members had been dismissed for disobedience, she had appeared as a Dictator before a "Daughters of Light" group, and, according to a stenographic report, said:

"Don't any of you ever dare try to separate any of the staff from us again . . . I will drive every bit of viciousness right back into your bodies, and I have the power to do it. If you doubt my ability, just look at those who have just been dismissed. They are living in want, in dire need, and the same thing will happen to any others who cross us and this Work."

But soon a real crisis was to confront this feminine Dictator, who by such threats holds her people in abject fear of her alleged powers.

For during this Shrine class there was to occur an event which would test all the resourcefulness of this woman who had in a few years risen from mediocre harpist and bookstore saleswoman in Chicago to a position of psychic Dictator over the lives of thousands of her followers throughout the United States of America.

What this event was, and the effect of it, will be described in a later chapter.

CHAPTER 33

GEORGE WASHINGTON BALLARD FOR PRESIDENT!

Back in 1789 when George Washington took charge as first President of the United States of America, that personage—if we can believe it—was really the present George Washington Ballard!

Therefore, the reincarnated George has had a natural leaning toward the White House—and, if we can believe his published statement made at New York on October 21, 1937, *Guy Ballard's "Mighty I AM" has already taken charge of our government!* We quote:

"This day, I set My Legions into action in your government; in your city, the head of the finances of the world; to take command and bring all human beings into obedience to Me!" (pp. 24-25, Dec., 1937, v.)

Of course, the absurdity is that such wild claims should be found anywhere except on the inside of a mad house, but in this instance they were seriously uttered on the outside—and cheered by a hall full of fervidly patriotic Americans.

Encouraged by his audience's evident approval for him to take over the finances of the world, Guy Ballard reached out to take in the Supreme Court of the United States.

"I AM the Presence," said the present George, "which shall act in your Supreme Court . . . No longer shall human creation dominate My People! . . . I say to all destructive forces . . . 'Now, you shall face me! a Power with which you cannot cope! which you cannot harm, but which can make you helpless!" (p. 26.)

We cannot but wonder what the nine sober-minded

members of the Nation's highest tribunal will say on the day Guy Ballard's "I AM" formally descends to take charge of their Supreme Court. Their verdict must surely be that such a thing is slightly unconstitutional—even for people heaven-bent on "saving" the Constitution.

Luckily for our constitutional democracy, Ballard and his flaming "I AM" were in New York at the time and not in Washington; for in such a determined frame of mind, with the power of Saint Germain and the Ascended Host back of them, they might have taken charge then and there!

Mrs. Ballard, one evening at the Los Angeles class toward the end of a tirade against "vicious" officials in our government, raised her right hand in dramatic gesture and shouted: *"But George Washington still lives!"*

That statement was followed by thunderous applause, for these people knew their George Washington. There he was seated on the platform—and his face certainly should have been red.

A year or so ago, while the Ballards were in the east, Guy Ballard, his staff, and some of the other favored ones, journeyed to Valley Forge. There Ballard and his patriotic band walked over well-remembered ground, so he said, and explained how it all came back to him—how he prayed for light and guidance and relief for his famine-stricken, frost-bitten soldiers when his Continental Army was in winter quarters there.

Later, in the February, 1939, issue of the "Voice of the I AM," there appeared a vapid poem entitled, "WASH-INGTON, WE LOVE YOU," written by Mrs. Ballard. Facing it was a picture of George Washington at Valley Forge attired in a white-lined cape that looks like the one Ballard himself wears on the stage at "I AM" meetings.

Washington's birthday is celebrated with fitting and proper observances by this bewildering family of "I AM-ers." These people, however, for years have worshipped not a dead Washington, but a living one!

One evening in their hotel suite George Washington Ballard and the members of his present "staff" were looking at a picture of the well-known painting, "Washington Crossing the Delaware."

It brought back stirring memories to the present redoubtable George. He pointed out how certain of the most faithful members of his staff helped him to make the perilous journey through crashing blocks of ice and the raging river.

This staff member was the man with the oar, *that* one was the man at the stern, and so on with the rest of the staff, while of course Ballard himself was General Washington holding aloft the flag at the bow of the bobbing boat.

That this painting was but an artist's conception—and not so accurate at that—seemed to have been overlooked by the present George and taken as an absolute fact.

At the Washington class on Armistice Day, November 11, 1938, a little ceremony took place which doubtlessly gave new impetus to Ballard's presidential ambitions. We quote from the official report:

"When our precious Messengers, Mr. and Mrs. Ballard and Donald, walked out on the stage, they were welcomed by a mighty ovation. Then a huge Uncle Sam hat, fully 3 feet high, was passed up to Mr. Ballard. It was made of red, white and blue carnations, in stripes, a real Uncle Sam hat! He made an attempt to put it on his head, but it was too big!" (p. 2, Dec. 20, 1938, G. L.)

We should think it would be! It is surprising, too, that he would have the hated color, red, so near to him.

One afternoon a little over a year ago, Donald Ballard in company with one of his father's "staff" members, was walking down historic Pennsylvania Avenue. As the two passed the White House, Donald turned to his companion and pointed through the gateway to the President's quarters, saying:

"That man has no business in there. My Dad should be the head of this Nation right now!"

In the Ballards' official report to their Centers, under date of March 11, 1938, there appeared the following veiled statement as to the future destiny of the reincarnated Washington and his official family:

"You are familiar with the fact that it was our Beloved Saint Germain Who saved Washington and the Continental Army; and who established Washington as the first President of the United States of America. Unknown to anyone He has been training our Precious *MR. AND MRS. BALLARD*, His children in that long ago, to carry this 'Light' under His direction . . ."

Their people actually believe that George Washington Ballard and his wife Edna are being trained to bring a "New Government" into America, and it is no doubt flattering to these trusting souls to think they will have a part to play in it.

Campaign-manager Saint Germain at the San Francisco class on February 5, 1938, seemed to be quite sanguine as to the political outlook. We quote:

"I tell you, dear ones, *you are becoming a power in the world!* Do not forget it!" (p. 6, March, 1938, v.)

The Ascended Master "Mighty Victory," while speaking at San Diego, said:

"This momentum is just getting well into action now, but when another million people are pouring forth these Decrees, you will see something!" (p. 8, March, 1939, v.)

The "Queen of Light" aroused the patriotic I AM-ers in Kansas City by saying:

"As you, a body of more than four hundred thousand students, issue these Decrees, do you think for one moment that you cannot regulate the conditions; even in the requirement of the government?" (pp. 450-451, A. M. L.)

The "Goddess of Liberty," who seems to have given

General Washington a "vision" of the future, said while at New York:

"Know the accuracy of the vision shown Washington! for remember, *until the Ascended Masters TAKE COMMAND OF AMERICA, Washington will stand.*" (p. 466, A. M. L., our capitals and italics.)

The Ballard official report, calling attention to the patriotic bands of "Minute Men" organized all over the country, said:

"You will be interested to know how the activity of the Minute Men is expanding. At their meeting preceding the last Shrine Class 1800 were present. With the organ, drums and bugle blowing in their stirring 'Marching Song,' it is no wonder that men like to attend." (p. 2, Feb., 1938, G. L.)

These official reports are frequently in the nature of campaign speeches and "pep" talks. One reads:

"*Arise, Minute Men of America! Arise, Daughters of Light! Arise, Students everywhere! Rally around our great Commander-in-Chief!* Give Obedience to your Great God Presence. Hurl forth those mighty decrees . . ." (p. 3, Dec. 30, 1938, G. L.)

Another one says:

"*Awaken! Arise! Crusaders of old! . . . Joan of Arc, Washington, and the Powers of Light call you to sweep forward!* . . . Carry America, Mankind and the World to Victory! . . . Sweep onward in one Solid Phalanx of Light! Hurl forth your mighty Decrees! . . . Victory is nigh! Victory is here! Carry on!!!" (p. 4, Jan. 7, 1938, G. L.)

During a Minute Men's meeting at Washington, D. C., Guy Ballard was saluted as the "*Commander in Chief of the United States of America,*" which he acknowledged with his usual humility.

Later, at a Minute Men's meeting in Dallas, he waxed eloquent about the "vicious" happenings at the seat of the government, and shouted to the applauding group:

"As George Washington, I was head of my army, and if necessary, I will again mount my white horse and lead the armies to victory!"

On the afternoon of January 6, 1939, at the Shrine Civic Auditorium in Los Angeles, George Washington Ballard personally stated to the large audience assembled there, his remarks being also broadcast over the radio, the following:

"Why, we have," said he, speaking not so humbly, "over one million I AM students now; before the year is out we will have two million—and it only takes three million to govern the United States by Divine Order and Justice."

Back in 1936, Saint Germain told his audience at San Francisco:

"The Government—the New Government—will require your services ere long."

And, for years, his Minute Men with drums and bugle, with Archangel Michael's "Sword of the Blue Flame" in their physical hands, have been singing their patriotic Marching Song and hurling forth their decrees:

"Fill every office in our Land with Almighty Ascended Master FRIENDS of the Light!"

Can there be any doubt who these "Friends" are, and the parts Guy Ballard, wife, and son had planned to play in the "New Government"?

He, George Washington! She, Joan of Arc! Their son, Lafayette of France!

What additional and amazing steps they took to consummate their desires will in the next chapter be given— and, then, the sudden and unexpected sequel to it all!

CHAPTER 34

DEATH-BLASTS OVER THE WHITE HOUSE

It is very evident from what has gone before that the self-proclaimed George Washington, his wife, and son, have certain irrepressible ambitions to occupy the White House and bring a "New Government" into America.

Their methods of installing themselves there will doubtless not meet with the approval of the present occupants of the White House—nor indeed the approval of really patriotic Americans who believe in a representative government and not in a form of witchcraft.

Here is described the most fantastic plan of dictatorship over the lives and liberties of others ever recorded in American history.

For five years the Ballard "Death Decrees" have been hurled forth day and night in an effort to *"blast," "dissolve,"* and *"annihilate"* anyone who would interfere in any way with their plans to bring in a weird sort of government in America—a government of the "Ascended Masters" and their "Friends."

High officials of the present government, who might stand in their way of getting into power, have been especially singled out as their victims in a strange species of witchcraft.

As proof of this, we now quote from one of their official *"Staff Dictations."*

These dictations are very private and secret. The staff members are warned never to reveal them to a living soul, and to "keep them under lock and key."

The one to be quoted from is in mimeograph form, dated August 17, 1938, and is headed: "SAINT GERMAIN'S TALK TO THE STAFF—YOSEMITE."

The following note is attached:

"This has not been edited and is for the Staff use only. Please keep it carefully guarded and under no condition allow anybody to see or even know there were dictations in Yosemite."

This particular dictation is largely in the form of Questions and Answers. We quote:

Q. "Can't we consider destructive individuals the same as we consider discarnate entities as to free will?

A. "Yes, don't have any qualms of conscience, dear ones. When an individual has become wholly destructive, it would be a thousand times better to make the call and have them taken out of the body . . .

"I think it would be very great wisdom never to let it be known that you had dictations here, or even refer to your private dictations under any circumstances. Then there is not the desire to get hold of them.

"*And be very careful—all of you—in referring to ROOSEVELT or MRS. ROOSEVELT by name openly.*

"Be sure you don't do it; because you see, these sinister forces if they got sufficient hold of individuals in the government they might attempt to trump up charges to interfere with this work from the government standpoint."

Q. We should be careful what we say in the rooms for somebody might put an instrument in to get the conversations."

A. "Now please, every one of the Staff, take that firm positive determined attitude that nobody can put an instrument in the rooms where you are."

Now, why should the Ballards have been so careful to warn their staff members not to refer to President and Mrs. Roosevelt's names openly to others? Why all this fear about a dictaphone being installed in their rooms? Why all this secrecy in a so-called "Ascended Master" instruction?

We remind you, as shown by the preceding chapter, that these people for many years have had designs on the White House, and they want to bring into America a "New Government." They do not want any governmental investigation of their cult. And least of all do they want a dictaphone set in their hotel rooms to record such a meeting as will be described involving the President of the United States!

Reminding one of some aboriginal jungle where medicine men and their fanatical tribesmen perform rites and incantations to bring about the death of their enemies, we now record a secret activity of this cult which has taken place many times in their hotel apartment. It is no strange bit of fiction, nor did it happen in darkest Africa or some other aboriginal land where voodoo practices are still in vogue, but it has happened right here in civilized America —in New York, Los Angeles, Washington, and in other cities—and the truth of it is sworn to on affidavit by former members of the Ballard staff.

At night, following their class meetings, the Ballards and their staff many times would congregate in secret conclave in Mrs. Ballard's hotel apartment.

They formed a circle around the room, with, so far as possible, a man and a woman alternating.

In the center of the circle would be a stand or table upon which had been placed a chalice or a gilded goblet containing a few odd gold trinkets and coins—put there no doubt for some magical reason.

Upon this chalice would be placed a list of names. It was a "black list"—*names of people they wanted destroyed!*

Then still standing in the circle around the magic urn with its list of persons to be destroyed, they would raise their hands and thrust them rhythmically back and forth as though pushing something away from themselves. This was supposed to represent the destroying or cutting power of Archangel Michael's "Sword of the Blue Flame."

Calling on their various "gods" and "goddesses," they would then issue the decree:

"STIFFEN ON THE CROSS OF BLUE FLAME ALL THOSE WHO OPPOSE THIS LIGHT!"

Then again pushing their hands back and forth with appropriate gestures toward the "death list," they would call aloud the names of *FRANKLIN DELANO ROOSE-VELT* and *ELEANOR ROOSEVELT*, and issue the decree to—

"BLAST! BLAST! BLAST! THEIR CARCASSES FROM THE FACE OF THE EARTH FOREVER!"

CHAPTER 35

DEATH ENTERS THE BALLARD HOUSEHOLD

At his expensive Vermont Avenue mansion near the edge of beautifully-wooded Griffith Park in Los Angeles, a white-haired old man lies dying.

It is the early morning hours of December 29, 1939; and at exactly 5:20 A. M. the Messenger of Death is scheduled to arrive and take this man into the Great Unknown.

Seven days previous, their seventeen-day "Mighty I AM" class had opened in Los Angeles, and the announcement had gone forth: "Mr. and Mrs. Ballard will conduct another class at the Shrine Civic Auditorium in Los Angeles."

But when the great Shrine class opened, Guy Ballard was not there.

Edna Ballard explained that because of a serious crisis in world affairs, *"Blessed Daddy was out with Saint Germain."* And her followers, psychologized into believing that "Blessed Mommie Ballard" never told one single blessed word that was not the truth, believed her in this as in everything else.

They did not know that Guy Ballard, broken in health and decrepit of body, had been half carried from his expensive hotel apartment in downtown Los Angeles and secretly taken to this big house at 2545 N. Vermont Ave., in the exclusive Griffith Park district of Los Angeles.

They did not know that instead of being out on some "world service" with Saint Germain, Guy Ballard was waiting to keep his last appointment on earth—the one with the grim Messenger.

During his nine days residence in this house, Guy Ballard's condition had become steadily and progressively worse. Neither Edna Ballard, "Saint Germain," nor any other member of the "Ascended Host," could relieve the pain in his body or reduce the tremendous swelling in his abdomen which was gradually but surely taking his life.

Two days before the appointment with Death, a surgeon was hastily summoned. He came with his instruments and performed an abdominal operation on the body of this man—a man who for years had claimed to have a body of "Immortal Endurance," and who said over and over again that his was a *different* and more *perfect* body than the bodies of other men.

But neither the surgeon nor any other material or spiritual aid could keep the Messenger away.

And here on his death-bed, in the early morning hours of December 29, 1939, Guy Ballard, "Accredited Messenger of the Ascended Masters" and co-originator of the Mighty I AM movement, was soon to be called to render an account of his sixty-one years and five months of earth life.

Perhaps already, as he lies there in a comatose condition, the Scroll of Life, like a great panorama, unfolds before his eyes, bringing vivid pictures of his good and bad deeds done in the life now closing.

The pictures go racing by . . . his early contacts with "Masters" . . . his travels to mountain tops in search of gold . . . the gold stock-selling deals in Chicago . . . the years spent as a fugitive from justice . . . his refuge in Los Angeles . . . his secret return to Chicago . . . the re-union with his wife . . . the dawn of their great metaphysical idea . . . the piecing together of their books . . . the secret classes in Chicago . . . the start of their great "Mighty I AM" movement . . . the applauding audiences . . . their Messianic claims . . . the blasting of their enemies . . . their

White House ambitions . . . the death-blasts at the First
Lady of the Land . . . their death-decrees against the President of the United States.

And now, this last scene of all. Here in this big mansion near Los Angeles' wooded park, Guy Ballard, "Messenger of the Ascended Master," but now deserted by his
Mighty Saint Germain, who had allegedly given him power
over the forces of nature—awaits his own rendezvous with
Death.

Is that grim Messenger there in response to the great
"Law of Action and Reaction" which Guy Ballard so
often said could not fail to operate in the lives of others
but would not affect his own life because "*no longer could
anything be recorded on his life stream*"?

Is it true that "What one sends out, will inexorably
return"? Have his own death-decrees, like some fearful,
gigantic boomerang, returned upon their creator?

The breath rasps, the heart action falters, and those
who have been waiting in that death chamber draw nearer.

When all was over, the mortician was notified that
death had entered that household, and he came and prepared the body.

The physician took out his pen and wrote on his certificate as cause of death—"*Arterio-sclerotic heart disease*," confirmed by X-Ray diagnosis of the heart, and, as
probable contributing cause—" '*Cardiac*' *cirrhosis of
liver*."

And on January 1, 1940, the body of Guy Ballard,
which assertedly in 1932 at Chananda's retreat in India had
emerged *unscathed* after remaining "two days and two
nights" in the "white heat of a great furnace" (p. 390,
M. P.), was taken to a Los Angeles crematory and destroyed by fire.

Thus ended the earth career of Guy Warren Ballard,
self-styled "Accredited Messenger of the Ascended Masters," who in the last seven years of his life had a meteoric

rise to a position of strange influence over the lives and destinies of thousands, and yet, despite his claims to "Immortal Endurance," died as other mortals have ever died.

．　　．　　．　　．　　．　　．

But to his thousands of followers, Guy Ballard did not die! They believe that death, in the usual sense, did not come to him; that instead of dying, he *"Ascended"!*

They believe that this "Ascension" was made voluntarily and that there was no suffering or disease in his body, which, allegedly, was not like the bodies of the rest of mankind.

They do not want to believe that Guy Ballard, after weeks of agonizing illness, died from a complication of chronic diseases. They believe exactly as Edna Ballard—considered by many as the real originator and sustaining force of this cult—has psychologized them into believing.

For three days, she kept the public and her thousands of followers from knowing that her husband had died. The usual obituary notices were withheld from the press, and only her closest intimates knew that Guy Ballard's physical body lay dead at this house in the hills. The newspapers did not get the story of his death until three days later.

Guy Ballard died early Friday morning, December 29, 1939, from the diseases we have enumerated, which fact may be confirmed by the official death certificate filed at the Bureau of Vital Statistics at Los Angeles. The record of his abdominal operation on December 27, 1939, is given on this certificate as well as his cremation notice.

The symptoms of his illness are given on the certificate as having begun "three months and two days" before death. This would place the beginning of his illness on September 27, 1939, at which time he was in his legal home of Chicago.

During the last part of this illness Edna Ballard made

it appear that "Blessed Daddy" was out on some important business with Saint Germain, and therefore could not appear at the Shrine class. But the fact is that Guy Ballard was so ill he could not possibly appear. His body was so swollen that he was forced to sit up in his chair instead of lying down.

Following his death, the body, bearing the record of suffering and the diseases which took his life, remained for three days on the bed, awaiting the "Ascension," which did not take place. Afterwards, it was, with difficulty, placed in an expensive pink-plush casket.

On Monday morning, January 1, 1940, a private funeral was held in that house. And there, over the closed casket containing the body of her *"Ascended-Master"* husband, Edna Ballard preached his funeral oration.

Following the funeral the body was taken to a Los Angeles crematory and consigned to the flames—hours *after* its owner was supposed to have made his "Ascension." For years the Ballards taught that the physical body itself had to ascend when the "Ascension" was made; yet, instead of it rising heavenward, here was the body still on the earth plane, being consumed by the flames.

Edna Ballard claims that her husband made his "Ascension" three days *after* so-called death. It is a strange commentary on this contradictory cult that in the same issue of their official magazine which announced to the world the "Ascension" of Guy Ballard, appeared the following alleged statement from the Ballard "Jesus," made November 30, 1939: "There has been lurking in many the idea that one may make the Ascension after so-called death; but that *cannot be accomplished* . . . " (p. 6, Jan., 1940, v.) Yet, the claim is made that Ballard *did* make the Ascension after so-called death.

The dramatic role played by Edna Ballard in perpetuating the hoax of this cult is without parallel, we believe, in the history of cultism in America.

During the three days following her husband's death, and during all the preceding seven days while the Shrine class was in session and her husband lay ill, suffering, or dying, Edna Ballard made her appearance every afternoon and evening—as usual—and her applauding audiences did not know the secret locked within her heart.

Some might say Edna Ballard is different from other human beings, that she did not feel the well of emotion which must have sought for expresion as she made these public appearances, while, all the time, her partner of twenty-three years either lay dying or dead. Only Saint Germain's "Little Dynamite" can ever tell what went on within her brain and heart as she kept her secret.

Donald, the son, broke down and cried at his father's death, but not the stoical mother and wife. Her own aged mother died in Chicago on January 2nd, the day following the funeral of her husband—but the classes at the Shrine continued "as usual."

Such is no doubt the effect of the teachings of this cult, whose requirement to its students is to *throw human sympathy out of their lives*. One of the Ballard "Ascended Masters," the great "Maha Chohan," said of Edna Ballard that he took "the precious child Lotus" under his direction *"because she was ready and willing to have every human thing ground out of her."* (p. 9, April, 1940, v.)

But despite Edna Ballard's efforts to conceal her husband's death from the public, the newspapers got hold of the story about noon on January 1st, and on the afternoon of that day the news of Guy Ballard's death was out. Many of the local and national newspapers ran news items such as the following:

Chicago Tribune (Special news item from Los Angeles, Monday, Jan. 1): "Private funeral services conducted here today revealed that Guy W. Ballard, founder and head of the Great I AM cult, has been dead since Friday . . . After a funeral oration by Mrs. Ballard, the former Edna Anna Wheeler of Chicago, who served as high priestess

of the cult, Ballards' body was cremated . . . Ballard was born in
Newton, Kansas, and gave up paper hanging about 25 years ago to
delve into mysticism . . . obtained large sums of money from his followers and lived expensively . . . because of his difficulties in Chicago,
Ballard promised to send the cows, pigs, and sheep which have been
slaughtered in the stockyards, to haunt the people."

Los Angeles Times: "Attracted a huge following across the
nation . . . preached that through 'thought octaves' he could defend
himself against all enemies, all evils . . . traveled in expensive fashion
and owned four canary-colored high-priced automobiles . . . used a suite
of rooms at the most expensive downtown hotel."

Chicago Herald-American: "Drew huge crowds to his meetings in
the Civic Opera House . . . unique among modern Messiahs . . . it was
estimated at least 50,000 men and women joined his movement in
Chicago alone . . . Followers of the cult were astounded when they
learned of Ballard's death."

With this break of newspaper publicity concerning her
husband's death, it was of course necessary for Edna Ballard to make a statement of some kind.

Therefore, on Monday afternoon, January 1st, just before or while the newspapers were appearing on the street
carrying the news of her husband's death, Edna Ballard
came once again before her applauding audience at the
Shrine class in Los Angeles—this time to make the most
dramatic announcement she had ever made in a seven year
career filled with sensational utterances.

Having previously intimated that there would be an
"Ascension" at this class, she said to these miracle-seeking
people:

"Our Blessed Daddy Ballard made his Ascension last
night at twelve o'clock from the Royal Teton Retreat,
and is now an Ascended Master!"

The audience, stunned for a moment at so marvelous
an event and the significance of it, came suddenly to life.
Applause rang through the large auditorium, and ecstatic
faces looked heavenward, for, at last, their blessed leader
had made his "Ascension," as he so often said he would!

"Our Blessed Daddy will come back," dramatically

continued the victorious Messenger, "and there will be a big temple in Los Angeles where he will some day appear in all his Ascended Master Radiance, wielding infinitely more Power of the Light Rays than before his Ascension."

Having thus counteracted at this large Shrine class the newspaper stories of the *death* of her husband, Edna Ballard proceeded in the next issue of her magazine to play up the "*Ascension*" idea to her followers throughout the country. In an article entitled: "OUR MESSENGER'S ASCENSION," she insists that her students be positive about this matter.

"When people of the outer world," she says, "are discussing what has happened to Mr. Ballard, please make it clear that *Mr. Ballard has made the Ascension!* [her italics] . . . He can wield Power in that Body which America needs right now; and He is doing it with no uncertainty . . . Make your statements with positive force; for I assure you I am telling you the Truth and will never tell you anything but the Truth . . . We have nothing to cover up." (pp. 30-31, Jan., 1940, v.)

Following through with this intention of not "covering up" anything (not even a beautiful sales idea), Edna Ballard, in the next couple of issues of the *Voice of the I AM*, instituted a thorough-going campaign to sell her Ascended-Master husband's colored *photograph*—and at prices ranging from $2.50 to $25.00 per photograph!

"The photographs of Our Beloved Messenger," says she, "have been definitely prepared and charged by Him and us to render tremendous Service to all who use them for contemplation . . . Contemplation of His Picture and calls to Him are bringing forth instantaneous answers." (pp. 41-42, March, 1940, v.)

Having guaranteed instantaneous results to purchasers of her deceased husband's photograph, Edna Ballard proceeded to guarantee similar results to her students by permitting them to listen to Blessed Daddy's "*Voice*"—sold on phonograph records at $2.50 per record! "If the students," she says, "will use them in their own homes every day . . . it will enable Him to charge tremendous Power of the Cosmic Light and Perfection into the individual and his world." ("Our Messenger's Voice," p. 45, May, 1940, v.)

Thus, even though her husband is dead or "Ascended," he is still of considerable value to the surviving widow in holding the blessed students and increasing the I AM revenue.

It is one of the extraordinary workings of this mercenary cult that, today, thousands of apparently intelligent people who ordinarily would judge a business deal on its merits, refuse to use their minds to analyze the numerous absurdities, contradictions, and money-making schemes of this "Ascended Master" organization.

Ignoring the easily provable facts of Guy Ballard's death, as shown by the death certificate and cremation record, these psychologized people believe just as Edna Ballard tells them. They do not want to believe, or, FEAR to believe, differently; and until they are able to become *thinking* individuals again, their minds, souls, and pocketbooks are mortgaged to the I AM cult.

We would point out to these students that in all the so-called "Ascensions" in the Ballard books certain changes to the body of the ascending one took place. The "hair returned to its original color"; the "flesh became the pink of perfect health." (p. 84, M. P.) Afterwards, the physical body "disappeared on a Radiant Pathway of Light." (p. 242, U. M.)

It was this kind of "Ascension" which Ballard promised his students he would make—and didn't. Trying to get around this failure in some way, Edna Ballard explains that the "Beloved Messenger . . . was given His Ascension under the New Dispensation." (p. 26, Jan., 1940, v.) We have, however, shown in Chapter 9, "The Ballard

'Ascension' Miracles," that this New Dispensation idea is all part of the same cruel hoax.

In her article entitled, "The Victory of the Ascension," Edna Ballard, referring again to her husband's "Ascension," stated: "Saint Germain and the Other Ascended Masters said so repeatedly that *His Body was not like the bodies of the rest of mankind*," and added: . . . "The proof of the Tremendous Cosmic Power He now wields is the hundreds and thousands of instantaneous answers to the calls of the 'I AM' Students all over the world . . . " (p. 34, March, 1940, v.)

Nevertheless, this man who claimed to have healed thousands and whose body was so different from the bodies of others, ended his life in utter repudiation of his own claims and teachings. His last days on earth were spent in agony and disillusionment, causing him to fling away from himself the picture of his own "Saint Germain" which had been handed him in an effort to help him in his misery.

These and many other facts, Edna Ballard has sought to keep from her hypnotized students, who do not want to look—or *fear* to look—at the record in this book.

But some day, when the Mountain of Deception becomes too great for them to bear, and the Goddess of *Truth*—the one "Goddess" they did not dare bring forth —gets a hearing, then the record left by Guy Ballard and his wife, Edna Ballard, will be here for them to read.

.   .   .   .

Guy Godfre Ray King Ballard, self-styled "Accredited Messenger of the Ascended Masters," co-originator of the Mighty I AM cult, and self-proclaimed reincarnated George Washington, first President of the United States— is *dead*.

But his widow, EDNA LOTUS RAY KING BALLARD, beloved "*Little Dynamite*" of Saint Germain, surviving co-originator of the Mighty I AM, self-styled "Accredited

Messenger of the Ascended Masters," and self-proclaimed reincarnated *Joan of Arc*, sainted Savior of France—still carries on publicly the cult's activities through her radio broadcasts, sale of books, charts, photographs, and other articles of "Ascended-Master" merchandise.

Her thousands of credulous followers meet today in secret classes dedicated to "Saving America"—closed now except to those who give unquestioning obedience to unseen "Masters" and their earth-plane "Accredited Messenger"—and with fanatical zeal look forward to the time when George Washington Ballard, their former "Blessed Daddy" but now Mighty *"Ascended Master"* who "wields tremendous Cosmic Power," will come forth to bring the "NEW GOVERNMENT" into America and fulfill Edna Ballard's oft-repeated prophecy: *"An Ascended Master shall sit in the chair at the White House!"*

And so, dominated by a woman dictator, this strange subversive cult which has deceived and hypnotized so many . . . broken up homes . . . brought about divorces . . . caused insanities . . . blasphemed Christ . . . propagated lies . . . enunciated doctrines of hate . . . instilled nameless fear . . . bound thousands to psychic "Masters" . . . sent *death blasts* at the President of the United States—still continues in the United States of America, land of "religious" liberty.

Strange, incredible, fantastic—*pathetic*—yet this is the true story of that most extraordinary cult, known as the "Mighty I AM."

p 53 book burning
54 —

Ascension
74

p 101 - see art on H Jemain
in Paris

Sex. 186

p 129 a medium
p 130 ¶ letter about G.B.

attitude to animals
II 189-90

p 134 list

p 189 - Mu

194 = to

227 clv

229-30 B

246 dea

Date Due			